Waterways Restored

by the same author

RAILWAYS REVIVED
An account of preserved steam railways

HOLIDAY CRUISING IN IRELAND
A guide to Irish inland waterways
(David & Charles)

Waterways Restored

P. J. G. RANSOM

FABER & FABER LIMITED
3 Queen Square, London

First published in 1974
by Faber and Faber Limited
3 Queen Square London WC1
Printed in Great Britain
by Ebenezer Baylis and Son Limited
The Trinity Press, Worcester, and London
All rights reserved

ISBN 0 571 10434 7

386.460942

~~36265~~
009638

CANALS
I.W.
ENGLAND
WALES

Contents

5

Maps

N.B. These maps are intended to locate places etc., mentioned in the text. They are *not* adequate for navigation, particularly on rivers. Navigation and cruising guides are listed in the bibliography.

Plates

Metric Conversion Table

1 inch	= 25·4 millimetres
1 foot	= 0·3048 metres
1 yard	= 0·9144 metres
1 mile	= 1·6093 kilometres
5 miles	= 8 kilometres approximately
1 pound	= 0·4536 kilograms
1 ton	= 1·016 tonnes

1 · The Background: Why and how waterways are restored

A salesman of weed killer, I have been told, sometimes becomes despondent about his task. He does it well—and then: 'Go away,' his former customers say, 'We don't need you. You see, we don't seem to have any weeds now.'

Restoring a waterway is almost as unrewarding. Do the job properly, and there is nothing to show for it. Just a navigable river, such as the Lower Avon, or canal, such as the Stourbridge, on which boats cruise without hindrance. That there is sufficient depth of weed-free water, and that locks function properly, are taken for granted. Neither of these waterways—one a busy independent navigation, the other part of the British Waterways Board's cruising network—shows much sign of its recent past: in each instance, a heroic struggle over several years, largely by volunteers, to reverse its descent into dereliction and abandonment. On these and other restored waterways, no trace remains of their former state: channels un-navigable from silt, leakage, reeds, weed, and in built-up areas junk from bicycles to bedsteads; overgrown jungly locks with crumbling masonry and rotten or missing gates; swing and lifting bridges immovable from neglect or fixed by design; and installations damaged, broken or burned by vandals.

I have attempted to relate their stories in this book, however. I also describe most restored waterways as I saw them in 1973 (or, in a few instances, a year or two previously), and include something about their maintenance and traffic. The reopening ceremony of a restored waterway is not the end of the restoration story but only (and Churchillian terms seem appropriate) the end of the beginning. Restored waterways need constant maintenance just as gravel paths need constant applications of weed killer, however clear they may appear to be.

What is or was the reason for restoring waterways? Of many reasons, not all of which apply to all restored waterways, the principal is that all navigable inland waterways are more and more appreciated as amenities, not only for cruising but for many other purposes from fishing to admiring the view. But there are more and more people, who own or hire boats, seeking places to cruise and moor. And then there are the canals' great historic interest, and importance in industrial archaeology.

Because of these reasons, charitable funds and voluntary labour are available for restoring un-navigable waterways which would not be available for doing anything else to them, such as abandoning them and filling them in. For legally abandoning a canal for navigation did not abolish it physically. Unlike a closed railway, it had no scrap value: no one would pay to take it away. Either the closed canal tends to be neglected, becoming an eyesore and a danger to life and health; or it is filled in, at great public expense; or it is left in a state of suspended animation, a water channel with its bridges lowered (again at public expense) for the benefit of road traffic, becoming usually, a constant drain on the resources of its owners. Or it is restored.

There is one reason—lest there be any doubt in the matter—for which un-navigable waterways are not, in Britain in the early 1970s, restored. That is commercial carriage of freight. Navigable waterways were made for trade (although pleasure traffic is very old-established), and trade survives in parts of Britain and flourishes on the Continent, where barges are much larger than those to which we are accustomed. Commercial craft on most British waterways carried between 30 and 100 tons of freight. On the Continent a barge carrying 350 tons is considered small, and modern waterways accommodate barges carrying 1,350 tons. It would probably be advantageous to develop a system of inland waterways in Britain able to take such large craft: but that is another story. The waterways I describe in this book are no longer, except to the most limited extent, a practical proposition for commercial traffic: their locks are too small, their bridges too low and their channels too shallow to accommodate barges large enough to carry economic loads.

I have aimed to describe in this book those canals and navigable rivers in England and Wales which became disused, un-navigable or nearly so, and which have in recent years been restored, wholly

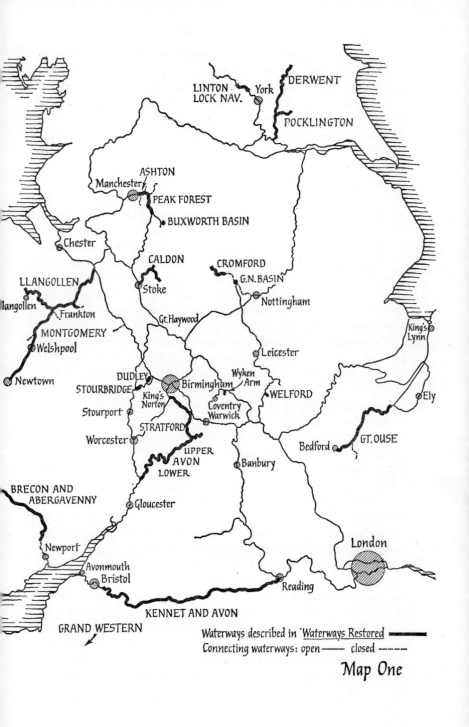

LINTON LOCK NAV.

York

DERWENT

POCKLINGTON

ASHTON

Manchester

PEAK FOREST

BUXWORTH BASIN

Chester

CALDON

CROMFORD

G.N. BASIN

LLANGOLLEN

Stoke

Nottingham

llangollen

Frankton

Gt. Haywood

King's Lynn

MONTGOMERY

Welshpool

Leicester

Newtown

DUDLEY

Birmingham

Wyken Arm

STOURBRIDGE

King's Norton

WELFORD

Stourport

Coventry Warwick

Ely

Worcester

STRATFORD

GT. OUSE

Bedford

BRECON AND ABERGAVENNY

UPPER AVON LOWER

Banbury

Gloucester

Newport

London

Avonmouth Bristol

Reading

KENNET AND AVON

GRAND WESTERN

Waterways described in 'Waterways Restored' ——————
Connecting waterways: open ————— closed ------

Map One

or in part, for navigation, or for which the principle of restoration has been accepted by the authorities concerned and restoration itself is far advanced. As that last long and cumbersome sentence suggests, it is a subject about which it is difficult to set precise limits. Railways are either open or closed, but waterways which became un-navigable usually did so by a gradual process of decay and neglect: they were still navigable to determined enthusiasts, armed with blocks and tackle and infinite resource, long after they ceased to be passable to the average holiday-maker. Legal abandonment, if it came at all, often came long after actual un-navigability, although this was not invariable: for instance the canal to Llangollen, abandoned statutorily in 1944, not only remained navigable but survived to become part of the BWB cruising network, and a very busy part at that. So the selection is to some extent a personal one. I have included, by way of contrast, one or two waterways of which restoration is still in the early stages; and also one or two which did not so much become un-navigable as have narrow escapes from becoming so.

To go further, to explain why some inland waterways became un-navigable, and needed to be restored, it is necessary to consider the history of inland waterways generally. Readers who reckon they know it all please bear with me for a few paragraphs.

Large rivers have been used as trade routes since pre-history. They were improved, and small rivers were made navigable, in the seventeenth and eighteenth centuries: shallows were dredged, weirs were built to retain year-round depth of water, locks were made for boats to pass the weirs. The work was inspired and administered at first by wealthy individuals or groups of individuals authorized by letters patent from the Crown; later, by commissioners appointed by Act of Parliament. On these river navigations travelled barges, which either sailed or were hauled from the bank by men. Horse towage came later.

Most of the artificial canal system was built in the late eighteenth and early nineteenth centuries, by canal companies incorporated by Act of Parliament. Early canals followed the contours of the land as far as possible, so limited were civil engineering techniques of the period; later canals crossed low ground by means of tall embankments and passed through high ground by deep cuttings, in the style adopted by the railways built soon afterwards. All canals needed locks and flights of locks to change level, tunnels to pass ground too high for cuttings, aqueducts to cross over valleys, rivers, streams and roads; and bridges, towpaths, quays, wharves, warehouses, staff cottages, maintenance yards, pumping stations and reservoirs. Buildings and civil engineering features had the functional elegance (or elegant functionality) of the period—and even today, on canals, one's immediate surroundings often contain more of the eighteenth and early nineteenth centuries than of the twentieth.

Though some canals were built to take barges or boats 14 ft. wide or more, many, including those in the Midlands which formed the core of the network, were built with locks about 7 ft. wide and 70 ft. long to take *narrow boats*. These vessels, carrying about 30 tons and drawn by a single horse along a smooth water-way, were a great advance on other means of transport: wagons, drawn by teams of horses, jolting over rutted roads; or pack-horses. The boats were owned by independent carriers (carrying by canal companies' own boats was a later development): canals were roads of water, analogous to turnpike roads. Over them, and over navigable rivers, the public had a right of navigation—a right of way by water, subject only to payment of tolls and use of boats of dimensions compatible with the navigation works—that is, locks, bridges etc. This right was granted by Parliament in Acts authorizing navigable waterways, in return for the many powers, such as compulsory purchase, that it gave to navigation authorities to carry out their works.

Canals and navigable rivers provided the transport which made possible the industrial revolution, and prospered—until steam power was successfully adapted to railways and, from the 1830s onwards, a country-wide network of railways was built. Rail transport seemed quicker and more economical than canal. Many canals came under railway control: railway companies wished to dispose of competitors, while canal shareholders got out while the going was good. Many (but not all) railways discouraged traffic on the canals they controlled or owned, and neglected the canals themselves; and, willy-nilly, sufficient canals became railway-controlled to sectionalize the network, splitting apart those waterways which remained independent.

There came, in the later part of the nineteenth century, a slight reaction in favour of water transport, particularly as people saw how canals on the Continent continued to be developed and enlarged (as they do to the present day). 'Our legislature surely was asleep when it allowed the Great Western Railway to appropriate the Kennet and Avon Canal, and thus bar the navigation to the Bristol Channel at its will by heavy tolls', wrote W. J. C. Moens in 1876, in a book which otherwise described a cruise through continental canals. By then, though, the Regulation of Railways Act 1873 had obliged railway companies to maintain the canals they owned, and to keep them navigable for 'all persons desirous to use and navigate the same'—a reinforcement for existing law relating to the public right of navigation.

So to be owned by a railway became something of a mixed curse to a canal. Some independent canals closed down, unable to meet rail competition, towards the end of the century, and some railway-owned canals, had they remained independent, would probably have done likewise. But other railway-owned canals would, like other independent canals, have remained busy.

The twentieth century brought the internal combustion engine. This benefited canals by enabling canal boats to be mechanized— but it benefited road transport far more. Between the 1920s and 1950s, transport, from being rail dominated, became road oriented; and canals and river navigations, despite spasmodic attempts to enlarge and modernize, continued generally to decline.

During the Second World War all the main railway companies and those canals and river navigations still considered to be important for transport came under government control; and when, in 1948, transport was nationalized, under the Transport Act 1947, it was those companies which had been under government control during the war which were affected. So far as inland waterways were concerned, this meant that the principal canals and some river navigations, together with the railway-owned canals, were nationalized; many others were not. Nor were carriers by water nationalized, except for canal companies' own carrying fleets.

Nationalized transport was administered at first by the British Transport Commission, acting through a series of public authorities known as executives. The formerly independent waterways passed direct to the Docks and Inland Waterways Executive; the formerly railway-owned canals went initially to the Railway Executive and were transferred, over a period of years, to the DIWE.

By this time much of the waterways system had either been closed to navigation, by Act of Parliament or other legislative process, or had simply fallen into disuse and dereliction. Much of what remained was navigable only with great difficulty. But some canals and rivers were still busy with trade, and inland waterways were still generally considered—when they were considered at all —only in terms of transport.

Despite this, a lay interest in inland waterways was emerging. Pleasure-cruising was long-established on certain waterways, such as the Thames. On the canals it was very rare, though also long-established. One of the few people who did cruise on canals was engineer L. T. C. Rolt: to describe an extensive cruise in 1939 over the Midlands canals in his narrow boat *Cressy*, of which the hold had been converted to provide living accommodation, he wrote his book *Narrow Boat* which was published in 1944. It was this book as much as anything else which opened people's eyes to the secretive, half-forgotten world of canals.

Among those who read *Narrow Boat* was author Robert Aickman. His interest in waterways had been aroused in the late 1930s when, during the course of visits to the Shakespeare Memorial Theatre at Stratford-upon-Avon, he had taken a walk along the towpath of the Stratford Canal as far as Wilmcote. He was puzzled: no boats, collapsing installations, weeds everywhere, many threatening notices in the name of the Great Western Railway. In 1945 he corresponded with, and then visited, Rolt. As a result, in 1946 the Inland Waterways Association was formed, with Rolt as secretary and Aickman as chairman. Aickman was to lead its campaign for the next eighteen and a half years. By 1949 the association had over 800 members; by 1960, about 2,500; by 1966, more than 4,250; and in 1973, 11,000. To limit members' liability, the association was incorporated in 1958 as a company limited by guarantee, with neither share capital nor distribution of profits. It has been registered as a charity.

The association's objects have been modified over the years, but in general have been, as in 1973, to advocate the use, maintenance and development of the inland waterways of the British Isles and in particular to advocate and promote the restoration to good order of every navigable waterway, and the fullest use of every navigable waterway by both commercial and pleasure traffic.

The emphasis is on *advocate*—in Parliament, in the press, and through publicity. The association has never taken over or restored a canal or inland waterway itself, directly; but many successful restoration schemes have grown up under its wing. The association's campaign, and the association itself, have had their ups and downs; but study of the course of events since 1946 suggests that were it not for the IWA there would by now be very little left of the inland waterways. It has been for the IWA a hard struggle—one not yet over—to slow down the decline of years, reduce its momentum, arrest it, and put it into reverse, to give waterways a future as well as a past. In the pages that follow I often chronicle beneficial changes of official attitude towards waterways in terms of official reports and Acts of Parliament: but these changes usually only reflected changes in public opinion brought about in the preceding years by a revival of interest in inland waterways, headed by the IWA.

By 1953 the IWA had already reached the conclusion that what was needed was a National Waterways Commission, which would not necessarily own or manage all the waterways, but which would have powers to ensure that all were maintained to the statutory standard and made fully available to all craft of appropriate dimensions—the commission to be composed of representatives of all interests connected with waterways: commercial carriage, public and private pleasure boating, water supply, land drainage, angling and amenity. The IWA has been promoting this idea, and various developments of it, ever since: by 1973 it was for a National Waterways Conservancy which would incorporate all navigable waterways including, it was hoped, those which were independent, that is to say, several of those described later in this book. Whether this aspect is wholly desirable is open to question, in my opinion, and in any case the IWA did not envisage an independent navigation authority being forced to hand its waterway over; but the basis of the original idea promoted over twenty years ago seems as valid as ever.

Later in 1953 the Docks and Inland Waterways Executive was succeeded by a Board of Management under the BTC; and on 1 January 1955, administration of docks was separated from inland waterways when British Transport Waterways was set up with its own board of management. Later that year came the report of a Board of Survey set up by the BTC which recommended that, while some waterways should be developed or at least retained, 771 miles of waterway which were either disused or carrying too little traffic to justify retention as commercial navigations should cease to be the responsibility of the BTC. This was the nadir: the report seemed to portend wholesale abandonments, and caused much controversy; and the following year the Government appointed an independent committee of inquiry into the future of inland waterways.

This committee, known as the Bowes Committee after its chairman, reported in 1958. It made positive proposals for development of much of the system but, overall, it confirmed—and this was accepted by the Government for the first time—the multiplicity of canal uses. It emphasized that to consider the waterway system solely as part of the transport network left much out of the picture: canals were important for supplying water to factories and farms, and providing land drainage; they were increasingly used for fishing and boating, and they added to the amenities of the countryside. Following one of the committee's recommendations, the Government set up an Inland Waterways Redevelopment Advisory Committee to advise on the future of waterways uneconomic for commercial transport. This, too, promoted the concept of multiple use.

With the Transport Act 1962, however, came a large-scale reorganization of nationalized transport. The functions and property of the BTC were divided among several new public authorities set up under the act. The BTC's inland waterways passed to the newly-constituted British Waterways Board (they had traded under the name *British Waterways* for some years previously). The act gave the board the duty to provide services on its inland waterways so far as it thought expedient, and to review the manner in which waterways not required for this purpose might be put to best use. It stated that the BTC's obligation to maintain its waterways, under the Regulation of Railways Act 1873, was transferred to the new board; but it also gave the board a temporary suspension (for about six years) of liability to maintain some of them: no legal proceedings were to be instituted or continued to enforce any obligation to maintain an inland waterway which had not been navigable during the six months ending 2 November 1961. This affected several canals over which right of navigation existed, which had become un-navigable, and for restoration of which the IWA and others were pressing. Nor, when a waterway was 'in any degree navigable' was the board to be obliged to maintain it in any better condition than it had been during those six months.

Following its statutory duty to review waterways, the new board produced first an interim report, in 1963, which again suggested that a multi-use policy might prove most fruitful, and then, in 1965, *The Facts About The Waterways*. This volume was the outcome of a long, hard and detailed look at its undertaking and in particular its financial aspects. It concluded that part of the board's waterways could still be run as a commercial undertaking—but it was a much smaller part than previous reports had suggested, for narrow-boat carrying had to all intents and purposes collapsed during the early sixties: with developments in road and rail transport, the loads which narrow boats could carry had become relatively too small, and the speeds at which they could travel too slow, to be competitive. (To be sure, even in the seventies a few narrow boats continue to trade, but in transport terms they are insignificant. Though it is delightful to see them—a canal without working boats is a frame without a picture.) For the rest of the board's waterways, *The Facts* contained a detailed, canal by canal survey which compared costs of complete elimination, reduction to a tidy water channel unsuitable for boats much larger than canoes, and maintenance for pleasure cruising. The conclusion was that even if every possible canal were to be eliminated or water-channelled—whichever was cheaper—there would be an inescapable minimum exchequer charge of £600,000 a year. The additional cost of using most of the non-commercial waterways for pleasure-boating was considered to be between £300,000 and £350,000 a year.

There is much of interest in *The Facts*, but one particular subject which it covers is worth considering here in detail. This is an analysis of what is needed to eliminate a canal—i.e. the opposite of restoration (and what has been needed for that I describe in later chapters)—and the cost of doing so.

On a rural canal the work would include de-watering the canal and breaking open culverts to drain its bed, piping incoming water discharges to nearby ditches, bulldozing the banks and importing fill, restoring boundary hedges and extending them across the canal, providing alternatives to water supplies taken from the canal, demolishing or filling in and if necessary piping bridges, demolishing and filling in lock chambers to prevent danger to children and animals, demolishing aqueducts, and making compensation for extinguishment of fishing rights. The cost of this, on a narrow canal, was reckoned at £6,000 a mile; on a wide canal, £9,000 a mile.

The IWA commented that from its information it thought these figures too low.

This is also an appropriate stage at which to consider how pleasure-traffic has grown on inland waterways. In 1951, the BTC issued 3,700 permits for pleasure-craft on its waterways. In 1965 the BWB issued 9,241 licences and lock passes for pleasure-craft; and in 1972 the total number of licences, registrations and permits issued by BWB to powered and unpowered craft was 20,269. (Because, for instance, some boat owners take out two or more short-term licences during a year, the actual number of boats licensed was slightly smaller—in 1972, 18,025.)

Each year since 1967 the BWB has carried out, on one day in summer, a count of pleasure-craft on its system. Boats are counted by the board's staff moving along waterways, so they inevitably miss some of those boats travelling in the same direction as themselves. Nevertheless the results are of great interest. The count covers, in England and Wales, 1,339 miles of canals and 317 miles of river navigations. In 1967, 6,747 boats were counted on canals, an average of about five a mile, and 4,183 on rivers (average about thirteen a mile); and in 1973, 13,453 boats on canals (about ten a mile) and 5,565 on rivers (about eighteen a mile). In other words, river boating was more popular, but canal boating was growing faster. (The figure for rivers was actually slightly lower in 1973 than in 1972, when it was 5,997; the 1972 figure for canals was 11,455.)

In 1965, the board's revenue from pleasure-craft licences was £81,600, which meant, according to *The Facts About The Waterways*, that it would have to quadruple, approximately, and given constant prices, to cover the cost of providing pleasure-boating facilities. By 1972, BWB pleasure-craft licensing revenue had reached £244,300, which looks like several steps in the right direction, even when inflation is taken into account.

The extent of hire cruising is also relevant. As early as 1947 the IWA was receiving on average half a dozen requests a week for information about hire craft—and in most instances it could only disappoint inquirers, for there were then very few hire craft operators, and very few boats. By 1967, however, there were 450 hire cruisers on the BWB system; and by 1972 the number had risen to 750. In 1973 the *Inland Waterways Guide to Holiday Hire* listed no less than 166 operators of hire cruisers on inland waterways, of whom 106 were on the BWB network. Many operators had more than one base.

In 1966 *The Facts About The Waterways* was accepted by the Government as the basis for development of a new policy on inland waterways. There followed discussions with all and sundry, a National Waterways Conference with distinguished speakers organized by the IWA, two white papers, and much debate, both in and out of Parliament; and then there was passed the Transport Act 1968. This act contained much that was good for waterways and one part which was resoundingly bad.

The bad part was that the public right of navigation over the board's artificial waterways was abolished. That section of the Regulation of Railways Act 1873 which obliged the BWB to maintain its waterways was to cease to apply. It was an action comparable to abolishing the right of the public to walk down the road.

A spokesman for the Conservative Party, then in opposition, gave an assurance that when his party returned to office it would restore the public right of navigation. At the time of writing it has yet to do so.

On the positive side, the 1968 act divided the BWB's waterways into three categories: *commercial waterways*, about 300 miles, which were to be principally available for commercial carriage of freight; *cruising waterways*, about 1,100 miles, to be principally available for cruising, fishing and other recreational purposes (for the first time, the BWB was given an obligation towards amenity —at a time, too, when cold economic considerations would have suggested closure of all the waterways in this category); and *the remainder*. The Minister of Transport was given powers to transfer waterways from one category to another: up to 1974, these powers had not been exercised.

The act obliged the board to maintain commercial waterways in a suitable condition for use by commercial vessels and cruising waterways for cruising craft—in each case, for vessels of dimensions corresponding to or less than those of vessels which used each waterway during the nine months ending 8 December 1967. If a commercial or cruising waterway had been restored or improved after that date, it was to be maintained for vessels of which the dimensions made them suitable for it.

The remainder waterways extended to about 600 miles, of which some 350 miles had been statutorily closed to navigation over the years, while much but not all of the other 250 miles had become un-navigable. Most of the BWB-owned waterways described later in this book came into the remainder category. The board's duty in respect of remainder waterways, imposed by the 1968 act, is worth quoting in full. It is:—'to secure that each of the inland waterways comprised in their [i.e., the board's] undertaking which is not a commercial waterway or a cruising waterway is dealt with in the most economical manner possible (consistent, in the case of a waterway which is retained, with the requirements of public health and the preservation of amenity and safety), whether by retaining and managing the waterway, by developing or eliminating it, or by disposing of it.'

In the board's annual report for 1971 it forecast that at least 240 miles of remainder waterways might be restored subject to satisfactory financial arrangements, 120 miles developed for amenity such as fishing and walking, some 60 miles retained for water supply and a hard core of 180 miles eliminated or incorporated in minor local recreational improvement schemes.

There were other important provisions in the 1968 act. Local authorities were given powers to assist, financially or otherwise, in maintaining inland waterways, or improving them for amenity and recreation. The BWB was given powers to enter into agreements with other bodies, such as local authorities or bodies 'having public or charitable objects' for them to maintain or for the transfer to them of remainder waterways. The Inland Waterways Amenity Advisory Council was set up, its functions (in a nutshell) being to advise the BWB and the Minister of Transport on proposals to add to or reduce the cruising waterways, and on matters affecting amenity and recreation on cruising and commercial waterways. In 1971, after lengthy and detailed investigation, the IWAAC produced a report to the Secretary of State for the Environment (the Department of the Environment having absorbed the Ministry of Transport) regarding many proposals for addition of remainder waterways to the cruising network—to the majority of which it was favourable.

Towards the end of 1971 the BWB became involved in Government proposals for reorganization of water and sewage services to meet increasing demand for water. The Water Bill proposed was the latest of a series of enactments, each of which had set up authorities with ever-wider powers. The previous act, the Water Resources Act 1963, had replaced river boards, which had been principally concerned with land drainage, flood prevention and fisheries, by river authorities which had wider powers to conserve water resources; they were also given powers to register and impose charges on boats on their waters where there was no other navigation authority, and to provide facilities for recreation. (These provisions were to be important in relation to restoration of the Great Ouse, described in chapter four.)

In the 1971 proposals, regional water authorities were to be set up, and the BWB waterways distributed among them, the board itself being disbanded. The thinking was that the BWB was no longer principally a nationalized transport industry, but was concerned more with other matters such as water supply and amenity. Following this line of thought the division of the Department of the Environment which deals with inland navigation and BWB affairs was transferred administratively in autumn 1972 from the transport industries side of the DOE to become one of four divisions in its Water Directorate. The 1971 proposals also envisaged relieving the taxpayer of the subsidy paid annually to the BWB and passing the costs of maintaining the BWB system on to water users through the annual budgets of self-supporting regional water authorities. Its maintenance would certainly have been only a small part of the RWA's responsibilities: and this, to the IWA, seemed to suggest not so much that the costs of maintenance would be 'lost' but that the waterways themselves risked being neglected. For this and other reasons there was much opposition to the proposals and when the water bill became law as the Water Act 1973 it was without mention of the BWB, which continued as before.

However, responsibility for navigation over some 500 miles of rivers, such as the Thames and the Great Ouse, was transferred to the new water authorities when they commenced to operate on 1 April 1974. The water authorities are given a duty which (shorn of legal jargon) appears to oblige them to make best recreational use of their waters, and a Water Space Amenity Commission is established by the act to advise on water recreation and amenity.

Following the Water Act, discussions started between the DOE and the BWB about the latter's future policies and finance. Included in these discussions were the future of remainder waterways and the upgrading of restored remainder waterways to cruising waterways. It seemed likely to me that further legislation was on the way, probably to deal with and rationalize the powers of navigation and water authorities—the 1973 act having covered organization.

So it can be seen that the survival of the BWB cruising network —let alone the remainder waterways—is still a very fragile thing, dependent on the goodwill of governments, the vigilance of enthusiasts and their organizations such as the IWA and, above all in my opinion, a continued rapid increase in the number of craft using it, to at least double the number at present. This quantity of boats, evenly spread, could be accommodated without destroying the peacefulness which is one of the system's intrinsic attractions.

It is against this background that the waterways described in this book have been or are being restored. Restoration of disused waterways has not been a movement on its own, but has been one facet of a greater movement to ensure survival of navigable inland waterways. Likewise, most restored waterways are not wholly separate entities, but are components of the national network.

Before going on to describe them in detail there are some other general points to consider.

The first of these is the organization of the British Waterways Board, the navigation authority for many of the waterways described. (Organization of each independent navigation authority is described in the appropriate chapter.) The board itself comprised, in 1973, a chairman (Sir Frank Price), a vice-chairman and five members, all appointed by the Secretary of State for the Environment. Next in line came the chief officers of the board: General Manager, Amenity Services Manager, Chief Engineer, Chief Estate Officer, Manager Freight Services Division, Secretary and Solicitor. At the end of 1972, the board had 3,081 employees.

On the engineering side, there were principal engineers at Leeds and Gloucester. Under them, area engineers were responsible for day-to-day maintenance and, where relevant, restoration of BWB waterways. They were assisted by section inspectors each in charge of forty to fifty miles of waterways. The following list shows the locations of area engineers together with those BWB waterways, covered by this book, for which they were responsible. (Other waterways described have independent navigation authorities.)

Wigan	Ashton Canal
Northwich	Peak Forest Canal
	Caldon Canal
	Montgomery and Llangollen Canals
Gloucester	Kennet and Avon Canal
	Brecon and Abergavenny Canal
Birmingham	Dudley Canal
	Stourbridge Canal
	Welford Arm, Grand Union Canal
Nottingham	Cromford Canal
Castleford, Leeds	Pocklington Canal
Watford	—

The central Engineering Services Department dealt with new works, mechanical and electrical engineering, and repair yards.

The actual management of canals was described so well in chapter three of the board's publication *The Facts About The Waterways* that I include the bulk of it, with grateful acknowledgement, as Appendix 2.

The board's accounts for 1972 showed a loss of £3,100,000 on operating waterways, after taking into account water sales (£976,000), tolls from commercial traffic (£524,000), and pleasure-craft licences (£244,300). The board has other minor sources of operating revenue, and profitable operations in warehousing, docks and properties. It received a grant from the DOE of £3,000,000 and its net loss for the year was £44,000. Total expenditure on operation and maintenance of waterways, including operating expenses, dredging, maintenance of buildings and structures, and administration, was £5,290,000, of which £2,616,500 was for the cruising network and £918,000 for the remainder waterways. In other words, the cost of maintaining and operating the cruising waterways which include wide and narrow canals and some river navigations averaged about £2,380 a mile (before taking into account revenue from them).

Most restoration schemes for BWB waterways, and many for those that are independent, are receiving substantial assistance, financial and otherwise, from local authorities. The change in the attitude of these authorities over the past few years has been remarkable. In 1949 the IWA was saying 'Local authorities seem to be the natural enemies of canals', and when in 1953 the DIWE proposed transfer of 600 miles of waterways, no longer required commercially, to local authorities, the IWA resisted strongly. In those days, local authority officials, not blessed with the IWA's vision of waterway potential, tended to regard disused or little used canals only as places for children to drown, rubbish to accumulate and rats to breed. Even ten years ago a councillor, or candidate for election, seeking popular causes to champion, would probably have proclaimed: 'Close the canal!' and 'Build the motorway!'

Nowadays he would almost certainly be against the motorway, and for restoring the canal. The change has come about gradually and was greatly helped by the Transport Act 1968 when for the first time local authorities were enabled to make direct financial contributions towards amenity waterways generally. (It is worth noting, though, that local authorities had and have a general power to incur expenditure in the interests of their areas or their inhabitants.) The act was followed up by two important conferences organized by the IWA: *Waterways in Planning* held in London in 1969 and *Waterways in the Urban Scene* held in Manchester in 1970—both were attended by many local authority representatives.

When a remainder waterway is restored the usual arrangement is for the cost to be shared between BWB, local authorities and voluntary organizations. BWB contributes the sum it is estimated that it would incur if it dealt with the waterway in the most economical manner (i.e. probably water channelling or perhaps filling in) in accordance with its obligations under the Transport Act 1968. The bulk of the balance comes from the local authorities, sometimes with Government assistance, but a substantial contribution comes from voluntary organizations such as the IWA and local canal societies.

For future maintenance of the restored canal, the BWB enters into agreements with the local authorities contributing towards

25

restoration that each will contribute towards any loss on operation (that is, the balance of expenditure after receipts from boat licences etc. have been taken into account) in the same proportions that they contributed towards restoration. In the event of the waterway being operated at a profit, BWB would pay out to the local authorities, again in the same proportions.

To raise money for restoration of waterways, the IWA runs its National Waterways Restoration Fund. This was opened in 1969 with a target of £50,000; by the end of 1972 it had raised £38,500. Some £14,000 had been raised by gifts under deed of covenant (the IWA, being a registered charity, reclaims income tax on these); donations, large and small, had raised £4,300; and much had been raised by other activities from proceeds of boat rallies (about £8,250) to sales of waste paper (£1,000) and other goods such as tea-towels and biros (£1,000).

The other important contribution that voluntary organizations make to waterway restoration (apart from promoting the idea of restoration in the first place) is voluntary labour.

Voluntary work on waterways started in 1950 with commencement of restoration of the Lower Avon Navigation. Initially concentrated in local pockets, it has expanded greatly in recent years in keeping with the whole waterway restoration movement. It has two remarkable features.

The first of these is the extent to which volunteers work for nothing for a nationalized authority, that is, British Waterways. The first full restoration scheme to utilize both BWB and voluntary labour was that on the Stourbridge Canal which commenced in 1964 (although volunteers had helped to repair a lock on the Kennet and Avon Canal in 1958); since then, voluntary work to restore BWB-owned canals has become commonplace. In its annual report for 1972 the board pointed out that it welcomed and encouraged voluntary work, acknowledging the marked improvements that resulted. It added, however, that it was not always possible to accept offers of help from individuals or small groups, and that work was best organized by responsible voluntary societies which, in conjunction with its own staff, arranged tasks in advance and ensured that adequate insurance, plant, equipment and protective clothing were provided for their members. It also expressed its appreciation of the co-operation of trades unions in connection with use of voluntary labour.

A great deal of voluntary work has also been done on un-navigable BWB canals in advance of official restoration schemes—usually with the authorization of the board but on occasion without (though no prosecutions for trespass resulted). Voluntary work in these circumstances was in the nature of a demonstration in favour of restoration by people who were prepared to show what could be done.

The other remarkable feature has been the growth of a national organization to co-ordinate the work of voluntary navvies: the Waterway Recovery Group. This had its origin in working parties on various waterways organized by the London and Home Counties Branch of the IWA from 1965 onwards. The idea of a roving volunteer work force spread to other branches and other waterway societies. In October 1966 was published the first issue of *Navvies Notebook* (the name was subsequently shortened to *Navvies*) with Graham Palmer as editor, a post he continues to fill. Although *Navvies Notebook* appeared under the auspices of the London Branch (which subsidized its production for the first twelve months), in the first issue it was stated that it was hoped eventually to cover all voluntary work on the entire waterway system—a hope quickly realized. The principal function of the magazine has been to give details of all forthcoming voluntary waterway restoration work, with dates and organizers, and to report on its progress. Circulation, originally seventy, had risen by early 1968 to 400 and by 1973 to nearly 2,000.

Out of the organization set up to produce *Navvies* developed, in 1970, the Waterway Recovery Group. Its principal function was to co-ordinate effort, ideas, plant and money for voluntary waterway work. In 1973, the group was still evolving: being still loosely under the IWA umbrella, its structure was informal—no committee, and no officers except *Navvies*' editor and a treasurer. Its core was formed by these, two or three helpers, and the organizers of working party groups—and these numbered forty-five, of whom eleven were working party organizers for IWA branches and the rest for other waterway groups. The WRG had no members either —just workers.

For the benefit of voluntary navvies, the WRG supplied navvies' gear: waders, steel toe-capped wellingtons, safety helmets, work gloves, donkey jackets and more. These were sold at minimum prices—wholesale plus a little to cover expenses. Other goods such as canal ware decorated with traditional roses were sold to raise funds. The group was also receiving £20 a month from the IWA. An insurance policy taken out by the IWA covers injury to or death of volunteer working party participants and third parties. Many waterway societies, themselves IWA corporate members, join in the policy for a small premium.

The biggest expenses of the WRG are in tools and mechanical plant, both its own and hired. The hand tools of the navvy include shovels, picks and mattocks; saws, slashers and billhooks to clear undergrowth and cut towpath hedges; and grapnels and kebs (long-handled, long-pronged rakes) to clear rubbish from canal beds and lock chambers. The WRG has found trading stamps useful for obtaining such items.

As for mechanical equipment, the WRG itself had an expanding stock in 1973: three sludge pumps, four dumper trucks, two Smalley excavators (described shortly), four diesel vans, a petrol van, and a pickup truck. All these were maintained and operated by volunteers, and all, apart from the road vehicles, were circulating among individual waterway organizations to supplement their own equipment. Other plant was hired, usually with drivers.

To elaborate a little on plant: pumps are vital because, although most of the water in a canal can be drained off by opening the paddles or sluices at a lock, some always remains and if water cannot be removed from around volunteers clearing, for instance, a lock chamber, they shovel only mud in suspension—difficult and inefficient. Dumpers are perhaps the most useful piece of equipment for navvies: they are highly manœuverable, operate over rough ground, and standard models with a capacity of say 15 cwt. were costing about £500 new, £75-ish second-hand, or £10 a week to hire.

The Smalley 306/5 is a delightful machine—a small hydraulically-operated excavator powered by a 7·5 h.p. diesel engine and able to swing its bucket round through 360 degrees. It has two wheels, four legs and no normal means of propulsion (though it can be towed, as a trailer, at usual road speeds); it moves about its place of work by putting its bucket on the ground at full extension, raising its legs and then dragging itself on its wheels towards the bucket. The National Waterways Restoration Fund made a grant of £1,644 to the WRG in 1971 to buy one.

Larger plant is hired by the WRG. It includes loader-excavators such as JCBs which are multi-purpose machines, tractors with a loading shovel at one end and a hydraulic digger at the other; and larger hydraulic excavators such as those made by Hy-mac, JCB and Priestman, which typically reach up to 35 ft. and usually are tracked vehicles able to cross soft ground. Hire cost was about £5 an hour, plus delivery. With these, lorries have to be hired, with drivers, to carry away spoil.

The cost of plant hire is a big item for the WRG—it has been as high as £1,500 for a single weekend on a really big project. For it is notable that when the need arises, working party groups from all parts of Britain congregate to a specific job—the largest such operation, up to 1973, being *Ashtac*, when, over a weekend in March 1972, some 950 volunteers descended on the Ashton Canal, in the southern suburbs of Manchester, and cleared 3,000 tons of rubbish from it, to give the official restoration project a send-off. On lesser occasions, working parties from local canal societies often have an 'away fixture' on another waterway project. This provides valuable experience and a change of scene for participants. All the same, the WRG was finding by 1973 that waterway restoration projects were proliferating almost to embarrassment: it would have preferred only half a dozen big ones on which to concentrate.

The total work force of volunteer navvies available through the WRG was in 1973 about 1,500, and still growing. Typical day or weekend working parties attracted about thirty participants, male and female. Most volunteer navvies are young, though less than one-third are students. Very few roving navvies have boats—probably fewer than one per cent, for once a navvy does get a boat, its maintenance tends to take up the time he would have spent digging—though many hire or scrounge them for holidays; and boat owners and boat-club members do work voluntarily on waterways in which they have a specific interest. To go navvying one needs old clothes, wellingtons or preferably waders, and waterproof industrial gloves; and food, if it is a one-day working party, or, for a weekend, a sleeping bag and li-lo or camp bed (accommodation is arranged in village halls and the like), knife, fork, spoon, plate, mug, and a complete change of clothes. And the will to work—though without having to be a superman or superwoman.

Paid occupations of volunteer navvies range from doctors, law-yers and computer engineers to postmen, policemen, railway-men and printers—almost every imaginable occupation except, unfortunately, craftsmen skilled in appropriate trades. And every weekend, up and down the country, they are to be found on the beds of canals and deep in the chambers of locks, mud up to the eyebrows, living up to the motto on those badges which the WRG sells to raise funds: 'I dig canals'.

2 · Shakespeare's Avon and the Stratford Canal

The Lower Avon

A long line of gleaming white glass-fibre cruisers rested at moorings, and from the water's edge neat lawns shaded by trees and brightened by flower beds stretched back to a wooded hillside. On the river other craft passed frequently to and fro, some of them privately-owned cruisers like those moored, others hired, others again narrow beam craft from the canals. When I have cruised on the River Avon, in 1973 as in 1970, I have launched my boat at Sankey Marine, downstream from Evesham, to find in these pleasant surroundings what was typical of the Lower Avon as a whole: a flourishing, well-kept river navigation, which flowed through pleasanter-than-average surroundings. High water levels and a district hilly for the Midlands enabled the scenery to be viewed over the banks: a land of hills, woods, meadows and extensive orchards; and interspersed with these, many boatyards, permanent moorings and riverside pubs and restaurants.

Writing in *Railways Revived* of the Talyllyn Railway I commented that its present air of comfortable prosperity gave no indication of the effort which had been needed to achieve it. The same is true of the Lower Avon. The two undertakings have other points of similarity: each was the object of the first scheme in its respective field, of voluntary railway preservation or voluntary waterway restoration, and each has, perhaps, developed in a manner slightly apart from the many which were to follow.

Among restored waterways, however, I found that the Lower Avon had two other distinctions: it is a navigation administered and maintained principally by volunteers, members of the Lower Avon Navigation Trust Ltd. which is the navigation authority; and, with low maintenance costs and high but not excessive boat density, it is a financially viable undertaking.

To find out how this came about, it is necessary to begin at the

31

beginning. The River Avon became an early river navigation, made navigable from the Severn at Tewkesbury through Gloucestershire, Worcestershire and Warwickshire, past Pershore and Evesham, and upstream as far as Stratford-upon-Avon. This work was done remarkably quickly, between 1635 and 1639, by William Sandys who was granted letters patent by King Charles I. Probably Sandys was helped by the existence of mill dams, which in many places held back sufficient water for navigation and meant that he had only to construct locks past them; in some places he built not locks but simpler water gates or navigation weirs: a weir would be built across the river, with a gap sufficiently wide for boats to pass through; when boats coming upstream had passed it, they entered a short section of deep water and moored while a lock gate was closed across the gap. Several hours later the water level would have risen enough for boats to continue upstream over what were otherwise shallows—simple and cheap, but slow to use.

The river became a busy commercial waterway and the navigation rights passed through several ownerships; in 1717, on the death of the then owner, the rights for the Lower Avon, from Tewkesbury to Evesham, passed to one heir and those for the Upper Avon, from Evesham to Stratford, to another. Since then the two sections have never had the same navigation authority. The Lower Avon continued to be busy until the early years of the twentieth century; then trade declined and with it the condition of the navigation works.

Various proposals were made to put them in order, and the Lower Avon Navigation Co. Ltd. was formed, a private company which acquired control of the navigation and did repairs; but when about 1930 a private bill was introduced into Parliament to enable the LAN Co. Ltd. to increase tolls, it was rejected after opposition by local authorities and others. This left the LAN Co. Ltd. unable to derive sufficient revenue from the navigation to meet maintenance costs, so that the navigation works deteriorated badly and during the Second World War they became totally impassable above Pershore.

On to this scene, after the war, came C. D. Barwell, an engineer with his own manufacturing business, a Worcestershire man, and a boating man with a motor cruiser on the River Severn. In 1949 he decided to explore the Avon. He took his boat on to it through Avon Lock, Tewkesbury, with the aid of the lock-keeper (that was

1 Restoration potential: Devizes Locks, Kennet and Avon Canal. Compare with plate 12 *lower*, taken 13 miles away on the same canal on the same day in August 1973. (Author)

2 *Upper* Lowered water level on the Ashton Canal, immediately before restoration, reveals a linear rubbish dump. (BWB)

Lower One of the last un-restored sections of the Upper Avon, at Stratford. July 1973. (Author)

the only manned lock), and passed, with difficulty, through the next lock at Strensham. At the third lock, Nafford, he was defeated: although he got his boat into the lock, water leaked out through the bottom gates so fast that he was unable to raise the level enough to be able to open the gates at the top. Eventually, having decided to retire, he had the greatest difficulty getting his boat out of the lock again: water leaking though the top gates now made the lock very difficult to empty.

For the future of navigation on the Avon—and indeed on un-navigable waterways anywhere in Britain—all this could scarcely have been more fortunate. For Barwell was gifted with both determination and a knack of press-ganging others into helping him. He had also been reading of the activities of the IWA, which had been formed three years earlier. He joined, became a committee member of the IWA's Midlands Branch, and formed the latter's Avon sub-committee, becoming chairman. Acting through the branch, he purchased in January 1950 all the shares in LAN Co. Ltd., and became a director of it. The cost of purchase was £1,500—for, as Barwell pointed out to me in 1973, the right to navigate through seven derelict or nearly derelict locks, together with one rotting wooden lock-keeper's house.

Barwell intended that funds to restore the Lower Avon should be raised by public subscription—he had experience of fund-raising, and also of charitable organizations such as the Royal National Lifeboat Institution. He was also aware that the LAN Co. Ltd.'s attempt to revive the waterway in the thirties had failed in part because of public fears that, while the navigation remained in private hands, its revenue might be diverted away from its maintenance. To eliminate these fears a different form of organization was needed: a company limited by guarantee was the obvious choice, with the word *Trust* included in its title for good measure. So on 1 August 1950 the Lower Avon Navigation Trust Ltd. was incorporated; its original subscribers included C. D. Barwell and Robert Aickman, and Barwell became chairman. Soon afterwards, the trust succeeded in obtaining charitable status. This was all pioneering work.

Principal objects of the Lower Avon Navigation Trust Ltd., as stated in its articles of association (in more formal language than I use), are to maintain and improve the navigation of the River Avon between its junction with the Severn and Evesham (the

C

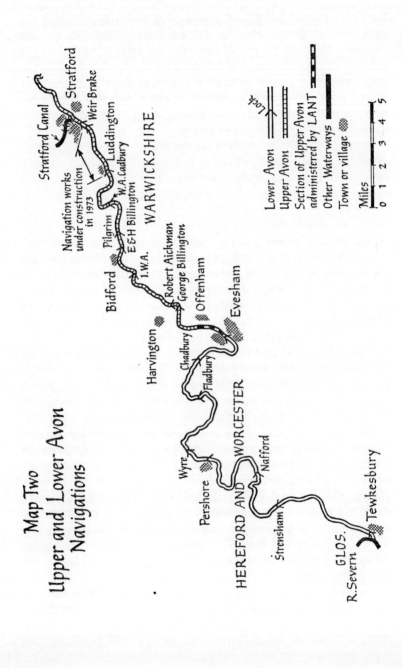

Map Two
Upper and Lower Avon
Navigations

Stratford Canal

Stratford

Weir Brake

Navigation works
under construction
in 1973

Luddington

W.A.Cadbury

Pilgrim

E&H Billington

Bidford

I.W.A.

WARWICKSHIRE.

Robert Aickman

George Billington

Harvington

Offenham

Chadbury

Evesham

Fladbury

Wyre

Nafford

WORCESTER

Pershore

HEREFORD AND

Strensham

Tewkesbury

GLOS.

R. Severn

Lock

Lower Avon

Upper Avon

Section of Upper Avon
administered by LANT

Other Waterways

Town or village

Miles

0 1 2 3 4 5

'Lower Avon'), to cleanse, scour, keep and preserve the Lower Avon, to make and repair navigation works and to acquire and operate the undertaking of the Lower Avon Navigation Co. Ltd. The latter object was achieved in February 1951, by which date the trust had raised sufficient funds to purchase the navigation rights from the old company (which was subsequently wound up: the IWA Midlands Branch Avon sub-committee was also dissolved).

Restoration of the Lower Avon, while maintaining its existing semi-navigability up to Pershore, was a long and arduous task. For a start, Strensham Lock became impassable only three months after Barwell had acquired control of the waterway, when part of the framework of one of the gates fractured. This involved him in expenditure of another £1,100; a new pair of gates was made by the Docks and Inland Waterways Executive, the start of a continuing association by which British Waterways has done this type of work by contract for the LANT. In June 1950 an IWA *Bulletin* reported that voluntary working parties would be formed to work at weekends on the locks and at such tasks as pointing brickwork, cutting back undergrowth, weed clearance and gate painting. Early the following year a participant in one of these working parties recounted in the *Bulletin* how he had helped to unload materials from a lorry for repair of Strensham Lock, and to deal with a tree which had taken root in the crevices of a wall at the entrance to the lock. Many bricks had to be loosened by crowbar and lifted out before the roots were accessible to be cut with an axe; then trees, roots, branches and pieces of old lock gate were burned. Among the volunteers was the divisional engineer of the DIWE, who made himself responsible for the bonfire. Apart from that feature, such activities now seem so commonplace that it is difficult to appreciate that they were then both unique and highly original.

LANT members went on to develop greater skills in waterway restoration and maintenance. The navigation was restored over twelve years, partly by volunteers, partly by contract and partly by detachments of the armed forces on training exercises. The principal works of repair and restoration—that is, those costing over £1,000—were these:

1952   Avon Lock, Tewkesbury. New downstream gates
        and repairs to chamber   £2,860

1953	Chadbury. Old lock rebuilt by Royal Engineers. Four new gates	£3,420
1954	Wyre Lock completely restored: new downstream gates, upstream gates replanked. Approaches dredged by dragline. Weirs and sluice gates repaired	£3,530
1955	Pershore Lock: work commenced to deepen it	£2,754
1956	Pershore Lock: deepened by three feet. New downstream gates, upstream gates replanked. Pershore old bridge, centre arch deepened by two feet. Water gate downstream from bridge demolished	£12,484
1958	Pershore Lock. Contribution to Severn River Board channel alterations scheme	£1,090
1958	Fladbury Lock. Chamber deepened by three feet. Walls of chamber rebuilt. Upstream gates replanked. Approaches dredged	£9,130
1961	Cropthorne/Fladbury. Water gate removed. Channel deepened for 600 yards up to Fladbury lock, new downstream approach channel, new downstream gates, new balance beams and paddle gear for upstream gates	£12,805
1962	Pershore weir and dam. Weir refaced, scoured area filled in, and other repairs	£3,234

As the navigation works were restored, boats were able to use more and more of the river; and on 10 June 1962 the twenty-six and a half miles of the Lower Avon from Tewkesbury to Evesham were formally reopened. But work did not stop there. The derelict Evesham lock, formerly part of the Upper Avon Navigation, was given to the LANT and was completely restored, which meant that boats could navigate for a further two miles to Offenham:

1963	Evesham Lock: new gates and landing stage, wall repairs, dredging	£8,327

and further work needed was:

1964	Pershore Dam. Steel piling approach wall to check severe erosion	£1,250
1965	Tewkesbury, Avon Lock. Removal of wooden building and construction of new brick lock house on piled platform	£5,799

Contribution towards rebuilding main dam, due
to foundation failure   £1,500

C. D. Barwell remained chairman of the Lower Avon Navigation
Trust until 1970. On his retirement from that position he was
awarded the O.B.E. for his work on waterway restoration.

Total expenditure on restoring the Lower Avon from near dereliction to navigable use was about £80,000. Much of this was raised
as a result of public appeals. Some came from subscriptions, and
from donations from members and well-wishers, often under
covenant. Other charitable foundations were generous, to the
extent of many thousands of pounds. The Ministry of Health
made a grant of £1,000 to the Borough of Evesham towards
restoration of Chadbury Lock, the next lock downstream from that
town. Local money raising committees were formed in riverside
towns: in 1952, for instance, Evesham's annual carnival (a mile-
long procession of tableaux) raised £500 for the trust. In 1957 the
trust successfully claimed an annuity of £400 a year from the
British Transport Commission: the amount had been awarded by
Parliament in 1793 to the owner of the Lower Avon Navigation in
perpetuity from the then new Worcester and Birmingham Canal
Co., as compensation for expected loss of traffic. The BTC was the
successor to the Worcester and Birmingham company.

There was, too, revenue from tolls. For the first full year of
operation of the navigation by the trust, that ending 31 July 1952,
tolls amounted to £520. Most years have shown an increase on the
previous year, partly due to increases in traffic and partly to
occasional increases in toll rates. By 1962, annual toll revenue had
grown to £1,288, and by 1966 (year to 30 September), £2,361. In
1972, after implementation of a voluntary registration scheme for
boats, income from registration and tolls was £6,399, and in 1973,
after the scheme had become compulsory, income from this
source up to mid-October was £10,458.

The voluntary registration scheme for boats had started in 1970,
and became obligatory when the trust's by-laws came into force in
August 1972. These by-laws regulate use of the increasingly busy
navigation so that all may enjoy it with minimal disturbance to
each other—principally by imposing a speed limit (10 m.p.h., and
4 m.p.h. past moored craft), safety requirements for boats and
their use, and registration of vessels. They were the outcome of

37

seven years of research and discussion, and were made by the trust, and confirmed by the Secretary of State for the Environment, under powers granted by section 113 of the Transport Act 1968—the trust had originally envisaged that it would have to obtain (at great expense) a private act, and it was largely at its prompting that the relevant section was included in the 1968 act.

From county councils, the trust has in recent years been receiving grants of £300 a year from Gloucestershire (a small part of the river in and near Tewkesbury lies within that county) and £500 a year from Worcestershire. In 1973 Worcestershire County Council, recognizing that the trust had in effect created a 'linear water park' through the county, made a grant of £4,000 towards its upkeep.

In the year ended 30 September 1972 the cost of operating and maintaining the navigation was £5,143, which included repairs and renewals at £3,861. The total cost averages as little as £183 a mile, approximately; this is a remarkably low figure compared with British Waterways Board cruising waterways. It probably results partly from the small number of locks, and partly from the mainly voluntary methods of working. With other income and other expenses, the excess of income over expenditure for the year was £630. There is not always an excess: the previous year, for instance, had seen a loss of £1,258.

The Lower Avon Navigation Trust Ltd. is administered by a council of management. The council members are the directors of the company, and are elected by members of the trust for terms of three years. The maximum permitted number of council members is thirty-five; in 1973 the council actually had twenty-five. It was meeting four times a year; and it appointed sub-committees on which council members served and on to which trust members were co-opted. These were as follows:

Finance and General Purposes Committee: chaired by the treasurer who was elected annually by trust members.

Operating Committee: responsible for day-to-day operation of the waterway, including minor engineering works: I return to it shortly.

Works Committee: responsible for major engineering works involving contractors (such as dredging, repairs to weirs, and reinforcement of banks where liable to erosion). Each spring the Works

Committee did a two-day inspection of the navigation, and then allocated work either to volunteers or to contractors.

By-laws Committee: responsible for interpretation and enforcement of by-laws and, through a further sub-committee of its own, registration of boats.

'Avon News' Committee: responsible for production of the trust's quarterly magazine for members.

The trust had, in 1973, six paid employees: secretary, registration officer, assistant treasurer and three lock-keepers. *Part-paid enthusiasts* would be a more appropriate description, for the total remuneration of all six was about £2,000 a year. And while the first three officials were, in theory, part-time, the lock-keepers had very long hours of duty. During the summer season (mid-March to mid-October) the three manned locks were manned every day, by either the lock-keeper, his wife or a responsible deputy, from 9 a.m. to 1 p.m. and 2 p.m. to 9 p.m.

Lock-keepers do get a house, on a service tenancy. Even so, men who have sold their houses, spent several years as Avon lock-keepers, and then returned to other occupations, have found that any savings they have made through having a house with the job have been inadequate, because of rapidly-rising house prices, to enable them to repurchase a house as big as that which they sold.

The manned locks are Avon, Strensham and Evesham. Evesham lock was unmanned before 1972; the decision to man it was made as a result of restoration of the Upper Avon (described later in this chapter) so as to ensure that boats coming downstream to Evesham did not continue unregistered down the Lower Avon. A new lock house was built by contract, believed to be the first new (rather than replacement) lock house in the U.K. for half a century. It straddles a sluice race, the only available site, and is constructed with A-shaped frames of timber—a pleasing, modern and distinctive building.

The other five locks are manned on Sundays and bank holidays throughout the summer by trust volunteers. Behind that simple statement lies something of an administrative feat: to man five locks for, in 1973, twenty-one days meant that the operating committee's voluntary chairman had to find volunteers to fill 105 vacancies for lock duty officers. Since many lock duty officers take family or friends with them for the day, in the course of a season several hundred people are involved. As an additional complication, Pershore, Wyre and Chadbury Locks could only be approached by water, so owners of boats moored in the vicinity usually undertook these sites. To see something of the voluntary operation of a waterway, my wife and I spent a Sunday in July 1973 helping to work Fladbury Lock. Not a typical day, though: the weather varied from merely overcast to heavy thunderstorms, and we saw only eighteen boats through the lock all day. Another helper spent the intervening time fishing with a large magnet at the tail of the lock for windlasses—the large cranked spanners used to operate paddle gear, and for which deep water seems to have an attraction! He pulled up no less than seven—all of which went to the trust for resale to help the funds. The record number of boats passed through a volunteer-operated lock in a day is 173, and for eighty or more boats to pass through has become commonplace.

The custom of volunteers manning locks started about 1954 at Nafford, when the top gates were still in such bad condition that they had to be winched open, something beyond the ability of most boat crews. It was soon found, however, to be a valuable public relations exercise for the trust, as well as a means to check that boats had paid for use of the navigation.

Each lock, manned or unmanned, and the reach upstream of it, is looked after by a pair of volunteer reach masters from the Operating Committee. Among other jobs they creosote lock gates and balance beams, oil paddle gear, tighten the bolts that fix handrails and paddle gear in position, maintain the lock hut and make sure its contents are complete (lifebuoy, rope ladder, appeal board, by-law board, registration application book, billhook, broom, shovel etc., etc.), maintain mooring posts and landing stages, apply white paint where it is needed, cut grass and nettles, and generally keep the lock area tidy.

For maintenance, the trust had the tug *City*, which was purchased in 1963 from BWB for £600 paid by a consortium of members, and its usual tow, the 65 ft. lighter *Lantern*. When I was visiting the Avon in 1973, these two had recently returned from a trip, under command of the LANT's volunteer tug master, to BWB's maintenance depot at Worcester on the Severn, to collect new gates for Fladbury Lock. There was another maintenance craft, *Chestnut*, once an army refuelling vessel and subsequently fitted with a derrick and boom to lift tree trunks and sunken boats, and

there was also the work boat *Avon Jubilant*, then the property of
C. D. Barwell but since sold to the trust for what it had cost to build.
At Wyre the trust had a wharf with a 30 cwt. crane, and was about
to construct a maintenance depot. Much of its small equipment was
still stored in a barn adjacent to Fladbury Lock, or at Wyre Mill.
This is now a club, allied to the LANT and with many members
common to both, and forms a convenient centre for operations.

All volunteers on the Lower Avon were LANT members, so as
to be covered by its insurance policy. Most of them lived within
fifty miles of the river, and many of them were owners of boats on
it. The number of members, which was 450 by July 1951, the end
of the trust's first financial year, and 686 by 1955, was in 1973
about 1,100. Adult annual subscription was £1.

No description of the Lower Avon would be complete without
mention of the barge *Pisgah*. Operated by mill-owners to carry
grain from Avonmouth to Pershore, she ran from about 1918 until
1972. She was then sold, but in 1973 she was still on the river and
there were hopes that she might resume carrying. Another veteran
on the river was the passenger M.V. *Gaiety*, formerly a Thames
steamer and brought to Evesham (via the Kennet and Avon Canal
and the Bristol Channel) in 1929. She was still there in 1973,
though her passenger trips had ceased. It is curious that in recent
years there appears to have been a decline in the traditional river
passenger boat trade—the LANT experimented unsuccessfully
with tripping craft in the 1950s—but there has been simul-
taneously a growth in day-tripping by converted narrow boats on
canals. Day trips were still being operated in 1973 at the
Tewkesbury end of the Avon.

There have been privately-owned pleasure-craft on the Avon
for many years, but over the past few years they have grown
rapidly in number—and also in size of individual boats. A count
of craft on the river on Saturday 26 August 1972 revealed a total
of 1,392 vessels, of which 676 were under 15 ft. long, 685 from
15 ft. to 39 ft., and 31 over 39 ft., and a count in 1973 noted 1,429
vessels. But this figure is not strictly comparable to the previous
year's, for in 1973 the count was not made until 22 September. A
better indication of the growth of traffic is provided by returns
from Avon Lock, Tewkesbury, where in 1973 the average daily
increase over 1972 in the numbers of boats passing through the
lock during July and August was over 36 per cent.

Despite the high average density of fifty boats to a mile the river did not in 1973 seem overcrowded. Many permanent moorings are off the main navigation channel. The increase in the number of boats has brought a problem in lack of places to moor overnight; this the LANT has attempted to meet by reinstating sites of former villages' wharves as temporary moorings.

It is a little surprising that on this attractive river there were in 1973 only two operators of hire cruisers, though it was also visited by boats hired on the Severn, the canals and the Upper Avon. Most boats were privately owned, and their owners came from farther afield than maintenance volunteers: extension of motorways had made it worthwhile for people living as far away as Manchester to keep boats on the Lower Avon for weekend use.

The Lower Avon has wide locks, some of which are uncomfortably short for full-length narrow boats (they were built, originally, long before narrow boats were developed, for small trows, barges of a type local to the Severn). It has also been rather remote from the main canal system (though this was going to alter with the reopening of the Upper Avon) so although some boat owners on the Avon, I found, had narrow beam craft and would, at times, go off to visit the canal system, far more had wide beam cruisers; and while some of these were happy to use their boats as floating weekend residences, scarcely stirring from their moorings, others would sometimes cruise off down to the Severn and away out into the Bristol Channel.

The Stratford-upon-Avon Canal

Like the Lower Avon, the southern section of the Stratford Canal had an epic restoration story, which culminated in a reopening ceremony by H.M. the Queen Mother in 1964. Its restoration proved the point that voluntary effort could successfully restore canals, as well as river navigations, and could do so cheaply. But unlike the Lower Avon, it has not flourished since restoration, despite high hopes entertained at the time, and its condition, when I cruised on it in May 1973, was a disappointment. It was certainly much below the usual standard of a BWB cruising waterway —although, to be fair, the Stratford Canal, under National Trust ownership, is maintained much more cheaply. The success of the

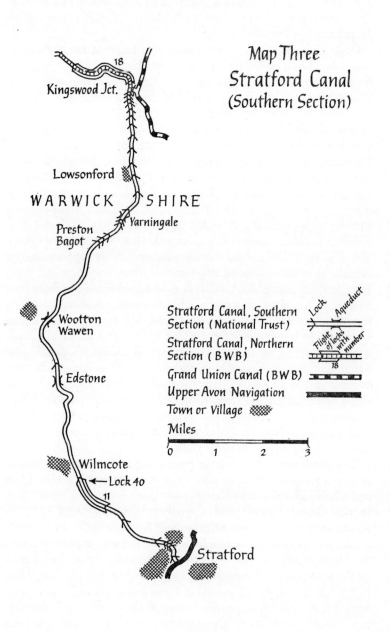

Map Three
Stratford Canal
(Southern Section)

18
Kingswood Jct.

Lowsonford
W A R W I C K   S H I R E
Yarningale
Preston
Bagot

Wootton
Wawen

Edstone

Wilmcote
← Lock 40
11

Stratford

Stratford Canal, Southern
Section (National Trust)
Stratford Canal, Northern
Section (BWB)
Grand Union Canal (BWB)
Upper Avon Navigation
Town or Village

Lock   Aqueduct

Flight of locks with number
18

Miles
0   1   2   3

restoration project was to some extent its own failing: its benefits have been felt elsewhere, in multiplicity of other restoration projects.

Once again, however, it is necessary to begin at the beginning. After the Trent and Mersey Canal was completed in 1777, and from it, at Great Haywood near Stafford, the Staffordshire and Worcestershire Canal southwards to the Severn, there came a period when many towns to the south-east of these two waterways desired connection with the successful new mode of transport. Canals were built in a south-easterly direction towards Coventry, Banbury, Oxford, Birmingham and Warwick. Stratford-upon-Avon was not to be left out of this: in 1793 an Act of Parliament authorized the Stratford-upon-Avon Canal and incorporated a company to run it. It had been hoped to build a canal from Birmingham to Stratford with a branch to Warwick, but canal-building politics eventually dictated that the Warwick and Birmingham Canal should be made on an entirely separate line (it eventually became part of the Grand Union Canal's route from London to Birmingham), while the Stratford Canal, as built, ran from King's Norton, five and a half miles south of Birmingham on the Worcester and Birmingham Canal, via Hockley Heath and Lapworth to Kingswood, from which point a link about 200 yards long was made to the Warwick and Birmingham, while the Stratford Canal continued southwards via Preston Bagot, Wootton Wawen and Wilmcote to join the Avon at Stratford. The twelve and a half mile section from King's Norton to Kingswood, which became known as the northern section, was complete by 1802; the continuation to Stratford, the 'southern section' of about thirteen miles, was not complete until 1816.

The northern section is level from King's Norton to Lapworth, at which place commences a flight of eighteen locks in about one and a half miles down to Kingswood; there is one lock on the link to the Grand Union; and a further thirty-six locks between Kingswood and the Avon at Stratford. All these locks are narrow, except for the final lock down from the canal basin at Stratford into the Avon, which was built wide to take barges from the river. Locks on the southern section come in groups: eighteen in the four miles to Preston Bagot, then a pound of three and a half miles separated by one lock only from another pound of three miles to Wilmcote, from which place there are seventeen more locks down to the river. There are on the southern section three cast-iron aqueducts dating from the early nineteenth century—a small one over a brook at Yarningale, a larger one over the A34 road at Wootton Wawen and a still larger one at Edstone, 475 ft. long and from 19 to 28 ft. above the ground; in the valley which it crosses are a road, a stream and a railway. Other distinctive features of the southern section are the 'split bridges'—in reality each is a pair of shelves bracketed from brick abutments, with a narrow slit between them through which tow-ropes passed without the need to detach horse from boat —and lock cottages with barrel-vault roof of semi-cylindrical brickwork: they were built, it seems, by canal builders who knew how to make bridges but were not too sure about roofs; so for a cottage they built a longish piece of bridge arch, put walls across the ends and inserted windows all round. Considering its proximity to Birmingham, the southern section is remarkably and pleasantly rural—as indeed is much of the northern section also.

In the middle of the nineteenth century the Stratford Canal came under railway control, and from 1863 it belonged to the Great Western Railway. The many distinctions of that concern did not extend to encouraging use of its canals. As a railway-owned canal the Stratford Canal was nationalized in 1948. By that date, although the whole canal was still a statutory navigation, traffic had faded away. The last occasion when a boat had traded to Stratford had been in 1933. From then on the principal function of the southern section had been to supply water to railway installations at Stratford; the water left the canal by pipe from above Wilmcote Locks. Below this point several pounds were kept dry and cattle grazed on them; above it, water levels were low and the canal became badly overgrown—at Preston Bagot, trees grew in its bed. Lock gates decayed so as to become unusable and the southern section of the Stratford Canal became almost derelict.

The northern section narrowly escaped going the same way. During the Second World War a lifting bridge at Lifford Lane, near King's Norton, was damaged by a lorry, and replaced, by the GWR, by a low-level steel bridge apparently fixed across the canal. So the northern section became impassable as a through route and silted up. Lifford Lane Bridge became an early *cause célèbre* of the Inland Waterways Association.

It took a question in the House of Lords to elicit the information that the bridge would be jacked up for boats to pass on twenty-four hours' notice being given. In May 1947, L. T. C. Rolt, then secretary of the IWA, and a party of members, having given due notice, set out along the northern section in his narrow boat *Cressy*. They were at first preceded by narrow boat *Bilster*, hired by the GWR to clear the channel: but this ran aground so frequently that *Cressy*, with shallower draught, overtook it. Approaching Lifford Lane the noise of a crowd gathered at the bridge could be heard 'from a considerable distance'. The bridge was indeed jacked up for the boats; and, when they had passed, jacked down again. The GWR decided subsequently to install a movable bridge, but there were many other occasions when the existing bridge had to be jacked up for boats before the Docks and Inland Waterways Executive installed a new swing bridge two and a half years later. Trading boats then returned to the northern section of the Stratford Canal, and nowadays it is a busy cruising waterway—though most of the crews of boats that pass Lifford Lane swing bridge, which has nothing obvious to distinguish it from others, are probably as ignorant of its history as was the author until the opportunity arose to study early IWA *Bulletins*.

As early as 1949 the Midlands Branch of the IWA was contemplating turning its attention to the southern section of the canal, and various attempts to form organizations in support of it culminated in formation of the Stratford-upon-Avon Canal Society in November 1956, at a time when the possibility of closing the southern section was being discussed by local authorities. The society's committee planned to encourage use of the northern section and to work for an improvement of the southern, trying to obtain permission for voluntary restoration work. It also decided that an attempt should be made to navigate the southern section using, since the locks were impassable, a heavy planked Canadian-type canoe that could be carried round them but could also cope with submerged debris. After tolls had been paid, the trip started from Stratford on 9 February 1957; it took six weekends to go to Earlswood, on the northern section, and back again.

Matters came to a head in 1958 when the Warwickshire County Council, backed by Stratford-upon-Avon Borough Council, announced that it intended to apply to the Minister of Transport for a warrant of abandonment for the southern section, under the Railway and Canal Traffic Act 1888. Its purpose was to enable Featherbed Lane Bridge, Wilmcote, then in very bad condition, to be rebuilt without the cost of providing for navigation beneath. The bridge carries only a by-road, but one which, since it leads to the house of Mary Arden, Shakespeare's mother, is well on the Stratford tourist circuit and carries much traffic. The act permitted abandonment of canals which had been disused for navigation for the previous three years.

The application prompted an immediate protest campaign by the Stratford Canal Society and the Midlands Branch of the IWA. This produced no less than 6,111 formal objections, sent to the Minister (with copies to Warwickshire County Council); to that of the Stratford Canal Society were attached the receipts for the canoe tolls of the previous year. And in May 1959 the principal objectors received a reply stating that the Minister had been advised not to proceed with the application because it had not been established that the canal had been disused for at least three years.

By then, much had been going on elsewhere. The IWA had been seeking a canal that was derelict or nearly so on which to prove its belief that such canals could, by use of voluntary labour, be put in order and maintained more cheaply than BTC figures suggested. The National Trust had become interested in preserving Inland Waterways, prompted by the IWA, by Robert Aickman, and by the chairman of its own executive and finance committee, John Smith, banker and sometime M.P. for the Cities of London and Westminster. After long negotiations with the Ministry of Transport and the British Transport Commission, it was agreed that the latter should lease the southern section to the National Trust for five years, with an option to take over the freehold at the end of the period. For this agreement, the authority of Parliament was required: it was contained in the BTC's annual act for 1960. On 29 September of that year the southern section of the Stratford Canal was transferred to the National Trust, along with all related rights and liabilities. These included a public right of navigation which, it appears, continues to exist over the southern section, since it was transferred away from the nationalized waterways before the 1968 Transport Act.

The official estimate for doing away with the canal was £119,000, according to John Smith (IWA *Bulletin* No. 67, November 1962), and for reopening, over £135,000. Towards restoration, the Ministry of Transport was prepared to contribute

£20,000 or half the total cost, whichever was the smaller, and the National Trust aimed to restore the canal for £42,000 (although no precise estimate was made: at that stage, no one knew what was to be done, how, or by whom, with what). The National Trust launched an appeal for £22,000; £10,000 was provided by the Pilgrim Trust, and at the IWA's 1960 annual dinner, promises totalling some £8,000 were received from among the 196 people present. The actual cost of restoration was eventually about £53,000. The National Trust paid no rent for the canal—on the contrary, during the lease the BTC and its successor the British Waterways Board paid the trust £1,500 a year, corresponding to the earlier annual loss on the section.

The National Trust appointed the committee of the Stratford-upon-Avon Canal Society as its local managing committee for restoration, with its nominee Christopher Clifford J.P. as chairman, and young architect David Hutchings, who had been active in the campaign for the canal, became its salaried general manager. The two lengthmen employed on the section by British Waterways transferred to the new management; one of them was shortly afterwards to retire.

The five-year lease was in the nature of a trial period towards the end of which the National Trust would have to decide whether to exercise its option to take on the canal permanently. It was decided to restore the canal over three years, as follows:

First year   Kingswood to Lowsonford, 10 locks, 2¼ miles
Second year   Lowsonford to Wilmcote, 9 locks, 8¾ miles
Third year   Wilmcote to Stratford, 17 locks, 2¼ miles.

Most of the work was done by volunteers. During restoration, seventy out of the seventy-four lock gates and all the 112 paddles on the section had to be replaced; thirty locks were given major repairs or rebuilt; and 200,000 cubic yards of mud was dredged from the canal. Working parties of volunteers came from IWA branches, canal societies, Boy Scout troops and the Civic Trust; regular volunteers developed skills in, for instance, fitting lock gates. Royal Engineers and Royal Air Force units gave valuable assistance.

Work was checked regularly by the Chief Harbours Engineer of the Ministry of Transport—the nearest official the Ministry had to a waterways engineer. Hutchings recollects that he was

3 *Upper* Skeletal gate and crumbling brickwork: Walbut Lock, Pocklington Canal, May 1973. (Author)

Lower May 1963 and part of the Caldon Canal has been piped instead of repaired. Nine years later it was restored. (Harry Arnold)

4 *Upper* Volunteers aided by JCB set about Park Head Locks, Dudley Canal, in September 1970. (Harry Arnold)

Lower A new weir is built across the Upper Avon at Luddington. July 1973. (Author)

conscientious and demanding, carried out frequent tests of materials and methods, and often gave useful advice, but at no time complained of the quality of any of the work.

The canal was dredged by dragline excavator, operated sometimes by direct labour and sometimes by contract. Cost of taking dredged mud away was prohibitive, so much was dumped on the towpath between temporary walls of planks which were later—an unpleasant task—recovered for re-use. This messy-sounding expedient has in course of time proved satisfactory: the mud dried out and consolidated and certainly by the time of my 1973 cruise no obvious trace of the operation remained, and the towpath was smooth enough for horses to draw visiting hotel boats. New lock gates were manufactured by timber merchants Wyckham Blackwell Ltd. of Hampton-in-Arden, not without difficulty in obtaining supplies of suitable oak. More than 200 tons were needed, which had to come from trees between 140 and 250 years old.

Restoration was not helped by the exceptionally hard winter of 1962–3, when, for instance, ice up to eight inches thick formed on the canal overnight. But work went on.

When restoration of the Wilmcote flight of locks commenced it was found that walls of ten of the lock chambers had bulged inwards, to leave the locks in places as little as 6 ft. 6 in. wide. This meant that the walls would have to be rebuilt. The unexpected work at first appeared beyond the resources available: but after negotiations with the Prison Commissioners, much of it was done by volunteer parties of prisoners from Winson Green Prison, Birmingham. The final big job was to remove 12,000 tons of mud from the canal basin at Stratford, which had been turned into a sort of ornamental lake by the borough council—to which the GWR had leased both the basin and the lock into the river with the stipulation that should canal traffic recover, they should be returned to use. During that lease a fixed footbridge had been built across the lock chamber (previously spanned by a swing bridge) rendering it impassable. This was replaced by a bridge at the tail of the lock.

So on 22 February 1964 the first test boat passed through to the river, having arrived from Lapworth. On 11 July came the royal reopening ceremony at Stratford, attended by some 10,000 people. To mark the occasion the Inland Waterways Association held its

National Festival of Boats and Arts, and 200 boats attended, after travelling down the canal. The royal reopening probably did more than any other single event to establish voluntary restoration of canals as an accepted principle. But for Hutchings the Stratford restoration had been, he says, 'the most appalling slog': volunteers were few and even when the final lock gate was being fitted, for instance, it could not be tilted into position because there were not enough bodies to provide the weight.

In 1965 the National Trust exercised its option and, without payment, the southern section of the Stratford Canal was transferred to it permanently.

What was the canal like in May 1973, nine years after reopening? Not, I regret to say, in my observation very good. Boat users were invited to report anything out of order to the trust: my list of defects ran to twelve items, ranging from absence of a balance beam from one of the lock gates to the condition of a collecting-box by the barge lock at Stratford. At that place, frequented by crowds of tourists, a notice expounded the canal story and invited readers to contribute towards its maintenance, using the box provided. But half of its lid was missing and when I looked at it, the box had collected only banana skins, choc ice wrappers and empty yoghurt tubs. (A new lid has since, I understand, been fitted.) The most common defect, in seven instances, was defective paddle gear (I retained, for a couple of months afterwards, a lump on my right wrist where it had been hit by a spinning windlass, the consequence of a deceptively worn safety catch which failed to function); but there was also much overhanging vegetation, which reduced the channel to the width of one boat on blind corners, and made it impossible to steer a bump-free course under certain bridges. A correspondent in *Waterways World* (August 1973), more particular than I, logged twenty-one defects in locks and paddle gear.

By this period the canal was costing about £11,000 a year to maintain and operate, or about £830 a mile. This is certainly cheap by British Waterways standards, especially considering the number of locks on the southern Stratford; but the low figure seems to me to be reflected in the condition of the canal. And only about one-third of the expenditure was covered by the canal's revenue—i.e. about £3,700 a year—which is derived mainly from tolls but also from minor sources such as fishing rights and way-leaves for telegraph poles. The balance was met by a subsidy from the National Trust.

The staff of the canal comprised, in 1973, the canal manager (responsible also for another National Trust property), a part-time secretary, a foreman, an assistant foreman who was an old-age pensioner engaged mainly in hedging, and a further man employed on general maintenance and practical liaison with voluntary working parties. The Stratford-upon-Avon Canal Society, with 170 members in 1973, played no formal part in running the canal, though it did help with money-raising activities and publicity. It has produced a most useful guide to the southern section, which in 1973 reached its fourth edition. It also concerns itself with the northern section, the Upper Avon, and indeed, with waterways generally.

The bulk of the labour force on the southern Stratford in 1973 was provided by Borstal boys (the change from adult prisoners having been made at the request of the prison authorities); other volunteers were provided by 'Acorn Camps' organized by the National Trust for youngish members, and by many canal societies, co-ordinated by the Waterway Recovery Group. The group has taken the southern Stratford Canal particularly under its wing and in addition to weekend working parties it organizes a work camp for a fortnight or longer each summer. Work on the Stratford Canal is welcomed by navvies as there they are able to do work requiring more skill than on BWB canals.

A weekend working party in which I took part in February 1973 is probably a good example of the type of work to be done on a canal such as the Stratford, and the way in which it is organized. The weekend was one of a series in which the task was to rebuild the by-pass weir and associated water channel at lock No. 40, Wilmcote top lock. These by-pass weirs, at all southern Stratford locks, enable 'maintenance water' to flow down the canal when paddles are closed (it is needed to replace water lost further down by evaporation, leakage and operation of locks—to operate a narrow lock uses 26,000 gallons of water). As built, they comprised a small weir near the top gate, its crest at the intended water level of the pound above the lock, leading to a narrow water channel running parallel to the lock and terminating in a corkscrew-shaped brick culvert which delivered the water to the lower pound. These culverts easily become blocked by flotsam, and, since water has washed away mortar from their brickwork, they tend to collapse: entering them to clear blockages is a most unpleasant task. They are gradually being replaced by open channels.

There was a further reason for rebuilding the by-pass weir at lock 40. Above it is the three-mile pound, which had been notorious for its shallowness ever since reopening. It was impossible to maintain the correct water level because of leakage. During the canal's years of disuse, water level had been allowed to fall, exposing, at the sides of the canal, the bed of clay puddle by which a canal retains its water. The exposed puddle dried out, developed cracks and was trampled by farm animals: when the water level was raised again, it leaked, and many of the leaks were very hard to find.

To help locate them it was decided to lower the crest of the by-pass weir by about one foot, and then to build it up by planks, one at a time. As the water flowed over the top edge of each plank, it would indicate that leaks up to that level had been cured.

The work was done by volunteers, helped only by one member of the National Trust's staff. Lowering the weir crest meant lowering also the level of the open water channel alongside the lock, so its floor had to be removed, and so did its brick walls, which could not be underpinned. All the closed culvert had to be dug out too, and before work could start the whole Wilmcote pound had to be lowered. The floor of the new open channel was made of concrete, and its walls from hollow concrete blocks. The blocks were stacked on edge and staggered from layer to layer so that their cavities matched, to make a series of tall cavities each the height of the wall: these were filled with concrete, mixed on site, to produce, in effect, a row of concrete pillars linked by the blocks surrounding them. The technique is doubtless familiar to those with building experience, but I have thought it worth describing in detail because it demonstrates how a wall that is substantial and serviceable (even if slightly irregular) can be built with minimum skilled labour. To complete the channel and help the walls resist caving in, cross pieces like small bridges were cast *in situ* of reinforced concrete. The whole job, a water channel a couple of feet wide, about 100 ft. long and 5 ft. deep at the most, absorbed about 1,000 concrete blocks, fifty tons of concrete, and the efforts of volunteers over seven weekends. With WRG representatives in charge to provide continuity, working parties came on the first weekend from the IWA London Branch Working Party Group and the Kennet and Avon Canal Trust, on the next three from the London WPG, on the fifth from the Surrey and Hampshire Canal Society, on the sixth from the K and ACT and the Grand Union Canal Society and on the seventh from the London WPG again. To add further to the pattern of co-operation, the concrete mixer used had been supplied by the Stratford-upon-Avon Canal Society, and an air compressor presented to the National Trust by its makers.

And all that is to be seen by passing boaters is a bit of new concrete work done to no obvious purpose!

This type of work is really deferred restoration rather than current maintenance, and with the latter, periodical working parties from scattered sources are perhaps ill-fitted to deal. What seemed to me conspicuous by its absence was a voluntary supporting organization with its sole object to assist in maintenance and operation of the southern Stratford Canal—and with members as dedicated to their tasks as are, for instance, those members of the LANT who maintain and operate its locks. Given such a group, I do not think any of the twelve defects on my list would have been present.

Pleasure-traffic on the canal was heavy in 1964, less so in 1965. Probably boaters were discouraged by reports of water shortage, justified in those first two years when although entitled under the lease to one million gallons a day, the southern section was dependent on its supply for the fluctuating amounts let down through the locks of the northern section from reservoirs feeding its summit level. In 1966 arrangements were made for a regular metered supply of 1,040,000 gallons a day to be taken from below the lock on the connecting link to the Grand Union Canal at Kingswood: this means that the adjacent eight-mile pound of the Grand Union has taken on the additional role of reservoir for the southern Stratford. The arrangement has alleviated the situation but not cured it totally—I write as one whose boat, during the descent of a series of shallow pounds, went aground at the tail of a lock, alongside and nose to tail with another boat trying to enter, and also aground. But that water shortage might have been caused by unskilled operation of paddle gear by a passing boater, and had certainly been put right a few days later. Even so, the southern

Stratford may not exceed its daily quota of water from BWB, and so has no reserve to meet sudden demands. These can only be met from the maintenance supply, which means that water levels, once accidentally lowered, take days or even weeks to recover.

The National Trust kept no record of the number of craft using the canal. I made my own count of craft seen on the move or temporarily moored, during my cruise from Kingswood to Stratford over two and a half days, and reached a total of thirty-two. Permanently-moored craft were few, the frequency of locks over much of the canal inhibiting short cruises of a day or less, but there were many house-boats at Kingswood. Day trips were run by passenger-carrying narrow boat *Linda* (which carried the Queen Mother on opening day) during the years 1962, '63 and '64, but she then moved away as a result of water shortages on the Stratford and better traffic prospects on the Grand Union at Cosgrove. Many boats run pleasure-trips on a short navigable length of the River Avon at Stratford, and in 1973 *My Lady Hilton*, a canal-type tripping boat, joined them, but operated out of the canal basin. She also occasionally operated up the canal to Wilmcote. *My Lady Hilton* was run by Western Cruisers Ltd., who were also for many years the only firm to offer hire cruisers on the southern Stratford, until a hire base was set up recently at Wootton Wawen by Anglo-Welsh Narrow Boats. The section is accessible to hire craft from many bases on BWB canals.

The canal is expected to benefit financially from the reopening of the Upper Avon Navigation from Stratford to Evesham, although it may see less use: instead of being obliged to make out-and-back cruises on the canal, visiting boats will be able to make it part of a round trip passing through only once—but would still make the same payment for a week's licence. It is to be hoped that circumstances and condition of the southern Stratford do improve, for despite difficulties, it is still a most attractive canal to visit, and where I have been critical, I have done so in the hope of stimulating the further support it deserves.

The Upper Avon Navigation

'Just follow the mud', they said at Luddington, when I asked where I might find Mr Hutchings. And there at the end of the trail of mud he was—David Hutchings, project manager of the new Upper Avon Navigation and restorer of the Stratford Canal, nailing up notices beside a road to warn traffic of mud deposited by lorries leaving the quagmire site of a new weir.

These notices, square sheets of wood with MUD painted diagonally across them, were nailed up diamond-wise:

so that they stood out to catch drivers' attention better than had they been made in the usual way:

$$\boxed{\text{MUD}}$$

In this small detail, it seemed to me, could be discerned the essence of Hutchings's waterway restoration: a flair for getting the most out of materials and methods which are simple, cheap and often unconventional.

Luddington was the highest point on the Avon which I could reach by boat from Evesham in July 1973, and work was in progress over the one and a half miles from there to Stratford.

It was about a century since the Upper Avon had previously been navigable throughout. The navigation passed through several ownerships after being separated from the Lower Avon; its trade declined after railways were opened in the district. In 1859 it was sold to the manager of the railway-owned Stratford Canal; from 1863 it was controlled by the Great Western Railway and in 1875 that company announced that it would no longer either take tolls or maintain the navigation works. Legal proceedings followed under the Regulation of Railways Act 1873, but the railway's argument was that under the Avon Act of 1751 it had no obligation to spend more on repairs than was taken in tolls, and judgement was made in its favour.

The navigation works then became derelict, though there were, over the years, various proposals for restoration. In 1951, the newly-formed Lower Avon Navigation Trust was already exploring the possibility of extending its work to the Upper Avon, and established an Upper Avon Committee in 1954.

The big positive step forward came in 1963 when, according to the IWA *Bulletin* published in May that year, a member who wished to remain anonymous had offered £80,000 towards restoring the Upper Avon. At that time navigation of the Lower Avon had been restored to Evesham and work was in full swing on the Stratford Canal. The IWA started to investigate the problems of Upper Avon restoration, and in 1964 formed an Upper Avon Committee which included a representative of the LANT. The LANT's Upper Avon Committee was disbanded.

The problems that emerged, and their eventual solutions, are best dealt with under three headings: legal, financial and engineering. To take the legal aspect first, extensive inquiries had to be made to establish whether there remained any claimant to legal ownership of the navigation—possibilities investigated included British Waterways Board and British Railways Board, both as successors to the GWR, the descendants of the 1859 purchaser, and even the National Trust as lessee of the Stratford Canal. Meanwhile the IWA had promoted a company limited by guarantee, the Upper Avon Navigation Trust Ltd. This later acquired from the National Trust a conveyance of any rights in the Upper Avon Navigation which the National Trust may have had by virtue of its ownership of the southern section of the Stratford-upon-Avon Canal. The UANT was incorporated on 26 August 1965 and subsequently became a registered charity. Its main objects are (in brief) preservation, maintenance and improvement of navigations for the use of the public, and to acquire, manage, maintain and improve the Upper Avon in particular. The number of members allowed for was 2,000. Chairman in 1973, as he had been for some years, was founder-member Robert Aickman.

When the trust started to restore the navigation it did so after negotiation with, and in co-operation with, riparian landowners, the Severn River Authority, local planning authorities and others. Once negotiations for purchase or lease of land to construct locks were far enough advanced, it needed to acquire powers to be a navigation authority. For this, a private bill had to be promoted in Parliament. It became law as the Upper Avon Navigation Act 1972, the process having cost UANT Ltd. some £2,000, and time and effort in proportion. The act is a splendid little document which kicks off with a reference to 'his late Majesty King Charles I' and imposes a right of navigation over the Upper Avon for 'all the Queen's liege people'. The act makes the trust the owner of and navigation authority for the Upper Avon Navigation and empowers it to charge tolls and register vessels. It also defines the lower extremity of the Upper Avon as 'the tail of Evesham weir'. Because the section of the navigation from this point upstream through Evesham Lock to the Bridge Inn, Offenham, had been restored by the LANT before the UANT was established, the two bodies have entered into an agreement that this section will continue to be managed by the LANT.

For general liaison between the UANT and the LANT there was a joint committee of members of the councils of each, and with its other neighbour, the Stratford Canal, the UANT had a personal link in that the canal manager, Major C. B. Grundy, has been a council member of the UANT since inception.

On the financial side, the anonymous benefactor's offer was increased to £100,000, to be made available on the basis of £1 for every £2 raised elsewhere. This he later handsomely amended to £1 for £1, and increased the total again, to £120,000. By late 1973 the UANT had raised about £190,000 more, though further finance was being urgently sought to complete the navigation. Of sums raised, the DOE provided £25,000 via the Sports Council, £12,000 came from the IWA National Waterways Restoration Fund, and the Countryside Commission provided about £5,000 for work within its scope such as landscaping, sowing grass and planting trees. Charitable foundations provided large sums and one family—the Billingtons—some £15,000; local authorities provided £2,000. Commercial companies donated or supplied cheaply equipment from welding gear to paddle gear.

Another important source of funds has been a scheme for donations under covenant. Unfortunately opinion in the UANT seems divided on the benefit gained from this scheme. Indeed I regret to point out that, while I believe all of what I have written about the Upper Avon to be accurate, in attempting to achieve accuracy I have been much hindered by the many inconsistencies which appeared in information obtained from my four principal sources—two representatives of the trust, the trust's own progress reports, and IWA *Bulletins*.

The covenant scheme is for *donations*, note, not *subscriptions*: membership of the trust had not been offered to the general public, probably from a desire by its council of eight members to ensure that they remain firmly in control, in view of the large size of some of the individual donations made to the trust under their administration, and from a reluctance to have their energies diverted from the task of rebuilding the navigation by the internal politics which might result from a large membership. A general membership scheme would have enabled those who put up the finance to have a formal say in how it was spent; whether it would have been more equitable, or enabled more cash to be raised in total, is a moot point. At any rate, in 1973 the trust had only about seventeen members, comprising the council, the project manager and certain well-wishers.

On the engineering side, the principal problem was that of water levels. Of the ten weirs on the Upper Avon in the 1870s, only four survived, and of these only two, at Evesham and Stratford, were still retaining water at the correct level for navigation. That at Stratford enabled the river through the town, and for about three miles upstream, to be used by large numbers of pleasure-craft; the section was reconnected to the main waterway system when the Stratford Canal was reopened. Lowered water levels elsewhere had resulted in improved land drainage and the Severn River Authority would not permit restoration of the river to its former navigation water levels.

As a preliminary to preparing a restoration scheme, the trust had an aerial survey made of the flood plain of the Upper Avon and tributaries, and an underwater survey of the river was made by the Severn River Authority, the UANT bearing part of the cost. The restoration scheme that was then prepared for the seventeen miles of waterway envisaged ten new locks (entirely new, the former navigation works having deteriorated so much as to be little more than a hindrance), six new weirs and a great deal of dredging so that the water level for navigation would be below previous usual summer water level. Nine locks, most named after benefactors of the trust, have in fact been constructed, and the locations of some of them, after lengthy and detailed negotiations with landowners and river authority, are not those originally envisaged. The locks are larger than those of adjoining waterways —the 'gauge' of the Upper Avon is about 17 ft. by 80 ft.—so that many boats together can pass each lock at busy periods. Dredging has had to be so extensive that the new navigation water level is in places below the level of the former river bed. Over 1,000,000 cubic yards of spoil has been removed, much of it very hard, and much heavy plant and some explosives have been employed.

David Hutchings was appointed salaried project manager and his methods have been an extension of those used on the Stratford Canal. No contractors have been employed, but plant has been hired with operators, and Royal Engineers did much work in the early stages. Prison and Borstal volunteers have provided the bulk of the unskilled labour, with other volunteer working parties at weekends co-ordinated by the WRG. There is also a very small band of regular volunteers. At the time of my 1973 visit, people working on the navigation (on construction, maintenance and operation) comprised only the project manager and his secretary (shared with the Stratford Canal Manager), three plant hire staff and six Borstal boys; weekends at that period were producing on average three or four other volunteers.

Preparatory work on rebuilding the navigation started in 1968; the first full-scale site operations in the early summer of 1969. Generally, work has proceeded upstream from Offenham, though it has tended to leap-frog from site to site according, for instance, to availability of land. After three locks and a weir had been built, remains of two old weirs demolished and much dredging done, at a total cost of about £95,000, a deep-draught test boat reached Bidford in July 1970. The section was formally reopened on 12 June 1971 by the chairman of the Severn River Authority. By the time of my 1973 visit all nine locks had been built and the river was navigable to Luddington; there remained one weir to be finished, another to be built (both had been completed by November), and some dredging to be done. During the year the trust was able to negotiate improved water levels.

Methods used to build locks have been unique and cheap; they have been developed by Hutchings, an architect who originally was without civil engineering experience, for use with unskilled labour. Walls of lock chambers have been made from sheet steel piling. At each lock, after the site had been cleared, two rows of piles to form the side walls have been driven into the ground, and anchored to further piles set about twenty feet back from the walls. The lock chamber was then excavated from between the rows of piles by machinery. The bottom of the lock was made from reinforced concrete with a minimum thickness of eighteen inches. Lock gates were all second-hand, nineteen of them coming from the closed Runcorn flight of locks on the Bridgewater Canal, which were donated by its owner the Manchester Ship Canal Co., and others from the Thames Conservancy and other navigations. Fitting lock gates is normally a skilled and lengthy process: so on the Upper Avon, the usual procedure was reversed. The gates were lowered into position and hung, and steel-and-concrete cills, and quoins (the vertical recesses of lock chamber walls into which gates fit) of steel piling, were then built to fit. Divergences from the general method were made at Stratford Lock, where the unusually deep walls necessary could not be anchored apart in ground which comprised silt and soft clay, and so had to be strutted apart by an overhead structure of steel girders; and at Pilgrim Lock, near Bidford, where the reinforced concrete chamber walls were built from hollow concrete blocks to try to find a way of building locks without plant and by volunteers—but with 40,000 blocks to be placed and 80,000 cavities to be filled, it was reckoned too complex, and too demanding in supervision, to be repeated. Upper Avon lock gates are usually opened and closed mechanically, often by paddle rack gear installed horizontally. Not only did many gates arrive without balance beams, but it is considered that mechanical operation is easier with these wide locks than leaning on a balance beam— and when *that* is difficult boaters, particularly those playing at working boatmen, sometimes slam gates by raising paddles at the opposite end of a lock, with consequent damage to gates and cills. The first locks to be built cost about £5,000 each: Weir Brake, the last, cost about £10,000, although by the time of its construction the trust was paying four times as much for steel as it had been earlier.

New weirs have been built by driving in two rows of steel

piling across the river, strengthening them by steel beams and bars, filling in between them with stone and capping this with reinforced concrete. Another big job was to provide a navigation channel through the bridge at Bidford, which is 500 (or more) years old. Its foundations, under one of the arches, had to be lowered about six feet; an arch near the bank was chosen for ease of access, and, with lowered water level, provides as much headroom as the former navigation arch, which was the tallest one, at the mid-point of the bridge.

The countryside through which the Upper Avon passes I thought pleasant without being outstanding—though I am unable to report on it in detail for most of my attention was taken up in following the navigation channel. This was dredged from the bank, and crosses from one side of the river to the other according to which was most accessible for machinery: where the channel passes demolished weirs, only part of each weir was removed to allow boats past, and the rest often remains beneath the surface. So concentration was necessary to follow the very detailed navigation instructions and notices on the bank. But the notices, too, were sometimes reversed ('Keep right' for 'Keep left'), a form of vandalism attributed to ill-disposed anglers. So it is only fair to add that when, in deference to one of these dangerously misleading instructions, I was steering my boat on to the remains of Lower Harvington weir, a friendly angler warned me away with gesticulations and shouts. The best solution to marking navigation channel and obstructions to it would, in my opinion, be buoys and beacons actually in the river, as on Shannon or Thames. In any event the trust intends to achieve good navigation depth everywhere, right across the river.

I made my own count of craft seen on the way from Offenham to Luddington on 16 and 17 July 1973, and reached a total of sixty-five, of which eleven were on the move (many of these being hire craft from Tewkesbury) and fifty-four at moorings. By that date the UANT had, during 1973, issued about 250 long-term and 500 short-term permits for boats. During the whole year about 1,000 craft used the river, producing an income of about £1,550. In 1972, the trust had issued about 200 long-term and 500 short-term permits, which raised about £1,000. In 1971, toll charges and sale of maps had raised £155—that was the first year in which there was income from such a source. All these figures exclude craft on the detached section of the navigation through Stratford, where registration of boats had not been enforced.

Cost of maintenance of the Upper Avon Navigation in 1972 was very little, perhaps £500 on additional dredging, bank protection, painting etc. It was expected that in the long term maintenance and improvement of the navigation, with payments to some of the people concerned, would need about £10,000 a year, or about £500 a mile on average. This was to be raised by boat registration, a levy on moorings (those who established moorings benefit from maintenance of the navigation), covenants and, possibly, amenity grants from local authorities.

For the future, it was expected that the navigation would be maintained, improved and developed by the same methods as have been used for restoration. The trust is interested, too, in making the river navigable upstream of the present limit, to Warwick, Leamington and a junction with the Grand Union Canal. This would link wide waterways to the east—Grand Union and Thames —to those in the west—Avon and Severn.

3 · To the West

The Kennet and Avon Canal

Pewsey Wharf, on a warm August day, resembled many another place on waterways popular for cruising. A wide canal, its condition appearing neither better nor worse than average, passed under a red brick bridge of the familiar pattern (although a distant background of Wiltshire chalk hills was less familiar). Along the bank, on either side of the bridge, were long lines of moored craft, past which other boats cruised at intervals, and the wharf itself was busy with people, working on their boats, going out on them, or just looking on.

But those with boats could not go far. Pewsey is on one of the navigable sections of the Kennet and Avon Canal, and the canal's condition ranged, in 1973, from full navigability in some sections to what could easily be mistaken for total dereliction in others. In between these (literally, for the condition of the canal follows no geographical progression, rather the different conditions of the canal succeed one another in bewildering confusion) were to be found sections in almost every possible state: navigable with difficulty, overgrown with weed, clear but inaccessible to boats, recently restored, being restored, nearly derelict but with hopes for restoration in the future. The canal is eighty-six and a half miles long and has 106 wide locks; sections navigable in September 1973 totalled about fifty-seven miles with twenty-five locks—though it is difficult to be precise, for navigability of a sub-standard canal depends so much on size and type of boat, and the determination of the crew.

In the ten years from 1963 to 1973, eighteen Kennet and Avon locks were restored (though some of them were not, in 1973, accessible from navigable pounds), and so were some twenty-eight and a half miles of waterway, with approximately eight miles more made partially navigable. This is a creditable performance, and the work represents, in total, a greater achievement than many other completed canal restoration projects. Yet so far as restoration of the K and A is concerned, it was merely the beginning of a project which was rapidly gaining momentum.

The Kennet and Avon Canal extends from Reading via Newbury, Hungerford, Devizes, Bradford-on-Avon and Bath to the outskirts of Bristol. The waterway in fact comprises a central section from Newbury to Bath which is artificial canal, with river navigations at each end: the Kennet Navigation east from Newbury to High Bridge, Reading (beyond which point the navigation authority for the final mile of the River Kennet is the Thames Conservancy, or Water Authority from 1974) and the (Bristol) Avon Navigation from Bath to Hanham Lock, below which lock the navigation authority is the Port of Bristol Authority. If complete, the canal would enable wide beam craft to pass from Thames to Bristol Channel.

Of the two river navigations, the Avon is mainly river with occasional locks, but the Kennet includes long sections of artificial cut. They were opened in 1727 and 1723 respectively, but remained separate until linked by the canal proper in 1810. By then, the Kennet and Avon Canal Co. had acquired control of the Avon, and later purchased the Kennet Navigation—since when the whole waterway has been known as the Kennet and Avon Canal.

The waterway passed through the green and pleasant counties of Berkshire, Wiltshire and Somerset. In addition to much of what I would describe as natural beauty were it not, in origin, largely artificial, it has many features of interest. On the Kennet Navigation section there survive primitive locks with sides of sloping turf. At Crofton, steam beam engines of the early nineteenth century pump water to the summit pound. Beyond Devizes a gargantuan flight of twenty-nine locks descends Caen Hill. Between Bradford-on-Avon and Bath the River Avon is crossed twice by high and handsome stone aqueducts, Avoncliffe and Dundas. Not far beyond these, at Claverton, there survives an 1813 waterwheel-driven pump to raise water from river to canal. In Bath itself, through Sydney Gardens, iron balustraded bridges and ornamented portals of two short tunnels make the canal itself an ornament to that pleasant formal city—while on top of one of the tunnels stands Cleveland House, stone built and Georgian, and once the headquarters of the canal company.

5 *Left* Hired excavator clears rubbish from the lock at Great Northern Basin in November 1971. Lock gates were recovered and re-used. (Harry Arnold)
Right A new lifting bridge is installed at Talybont, Brecon and Abergavenny Canal, in June 1970 to replace a low-level fixed bridge which had obstructed navigation for over 20 years. (Harry Arnold)

6 *Upper* Volunteers clean out the Montgomery Canal at Welshpool in October 1969. (Harry Arnold)

Lower New weir and lock at Roxton, River Great Ouse, before admission of water. July 1972. (Author)

The company was purchased by the Great Western Railway Co. in 1852, a condition being that the canal should be maintained for navigation. The waterway had been prosperous before construction of competing railways; subsequently traffic declined and so, after the railway purchase, did the condition of the canal. In 1926 the GWR announced that it intended to apply to the Minister of Transport for a warrant for abandonment of the canal; the proposal met much opposition and was dropped, the chairman of the GWR suggesting that the company would give the canal away to any body considered responsible by Parliament. None emerged, and subsequently some improvements such as dredging were made to the canal, but economies were introduced also, particularly use of short-life soft wood instead of oak in lock gates.

During the Second World War the canal between Bath and Reading lay almost disused, silted and weed-grown. After the war pleasure-craft started to reappear, struggling along with great difficulty and sometimes having to be towed through the weed by gangs of men from the maintenance staff. Condition of locks was bad, too: for example, in April 1947 the offside bottom gate of Hale's Lock, on the Kennet Navigation section, collapsed while the chamber was being filled and caused a 'Severn Bore' down the waterway. Despite all this, numbers of pleasure-craft slowly increased, and there were attempts to revive trade on the canal, cargoes of grain and salt being carried to Newbury.

On nationalization in 1948 the canal passed to the Railway Executive, and was transferred to the Docks and Inland Waterways Executive the following year. In 1949, also, the Kennet and Avon Branch of the Inland Waterways Association was constituted at a meeting in Newbury; this led to formation of the Kennet and Avon Canal Association in 1951.

At the end of May 1950 a stoppage was declared, overnight, because of condition of locks, which closed the Kennet Navigation between Heale's (or Hale's) Lock and Burghfield Lock until further notice. Since that date the Kennet and Avon has never been navigable throughout. Other sections gradually became un-navigable—Devizes Locks, for instance, were impassable by 1952 —and the canal entered a sort of twilight existence. Perceptible through the gloom, when looking back from twenty years later, were three conflicting forces: the natural forces of decay and deterioration, on a canal which had received only limited main-

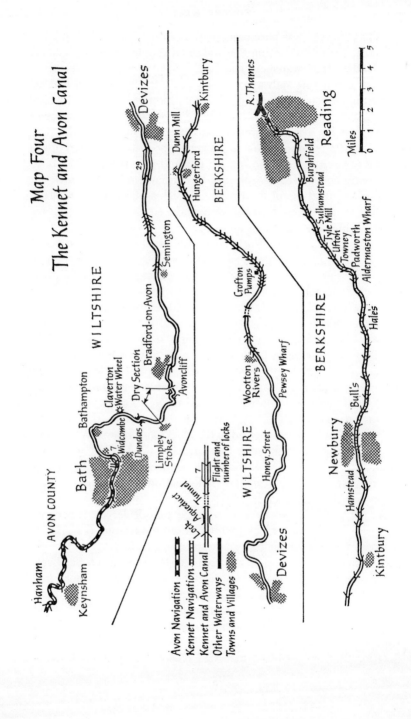

Map Four
The Kennet and Avon Canal

Hanham
AVON COUNTY
Keynsham
Bath
Bathampton
Claverton Water Wheel
Widcombe
Dundas
Limpley Stoke
Dry Section
Bradford-on-Avon
Avoncliff
Semington
Devizes
29
Dunn Mill
Kintbury
Hungerford
BERKSHIRE
R. Thames
Burghfield
Reading
Sulhamstead
Tyle Mill
Ufton
Towney
Padworth
Aldermaston Wharf
Hales
Bull's
Newbury
Hamstead
Kintbury
BERKSHIRE
WILTSHIRE
Honey Street
Wootton Rivers
Pewsey Wharf
Crofton Pumps
Devizes

WILTSHIRE

Avon Navigation
Kennet Navigation
Kennet and Avon Canal
Other Waterways
Towns and Villages

Lock
Aqueduct
Tunnel
7 Flight and number of locks

Miles
0 1 2 3 4 5

tenance for many years; the activities of the Kennet and Avon Canal Association and others who wished to see the canal reopened, improved and used (including lengthy legal actions by traders); and the intentions of successive nationalized navigation authorities, which ranged from limited repairs and proposals for repairs through minimum maintenance to abandonment as soon as possible.

The low point came in the winter of 1954–55 when the British Transport Commission's Board of Survey recommended abandonment from Reading to Bath; and the BTC sought the authority of Parliament for this. Extensive opposition to the proposal developed, and a petition to the Queen, in favour of the canal, was signed by 20,000 people living near to it. The petition was organized by the K and ACA. Opposition was successful to the extent of preventing total abandonment; instead, the BTC, while relieved of its obligation to maintain the canal, was not to allow it to deteriorate further; these arrangements were for an interim period until 1960, subsequently extended to 1963.

Gradually, things began to look up. Burghfield Lock, which had been reopened in 1952 and became impassable again in 1955, was repaired in 1958 by British Waterways staff and volunteers from the K and ACA and the British Sub-aqua Club. This is the earliest instance I have come across of volunteer work on the nationalized waterways system. The cracked cill of the bottom gates was broken up and a new one made.

Successive committees established to advise on the future of waterways began to view restoration of the canal, with voluntary support, more and more favourably, as did the successive nationalized navigation authorities. In 1961 the K and ACA resolved to reconstitute itself as a trust similar to the Lower Avon Navigation Trust. The Kennet and Avon Canal Trust Ltd., a company limited by guarantee and registered as a charity, was incorporated in 1962, its main objects being to take over the assets and liabilities of the association, to maintain and improve, as a charitable purpose for the benefit of the public, the Kennet and Avon Canal, either alone or jointly with other bodies, and to acquire all or any of the assets and liabilities of the British Transport Commission relating to the K and A Canal. In practice the trust has not taken over the canal, though it has purchased some of its ancilliaries, such as Crofton pumping engines and an old wharf building at Newbury.

In 1964 the trust, with others, initiated legal action for removal of girders which had been placed by Reading Corporation about 1946 under the span of Bridge Street Bridge in that town to strengthen it, and which severely restricted the height of vessels going up the canal unless the water level was lowered, a complicated business. The obstruction lasted for twenty years until the bridge was rebuilt in 1966.

In 1963, to show it meant business about restoration, the trust had created a fund with a view to seeking permission for some of it to be spent on rebuilding Sulhamstead Lock. This was then the first un-navigable lock upstream from Reading. The bulk of the reconstruction work was done in 1965: a new lock, designed by BWB engineering staff, was constructed by military and prison labour under BWB supervision, while the gates were made and fitted by BWB staff. Finishing and tidying were done by K and ACT volunteer working parties, and the cost, £6,875, was entirely raised by the trust, from voluntary contributions. In the meantime, Burghfield Lock, between Sulhamstead and Reading, had again become impassable: a new lock was built by BWB at its own expense and the two locks were officially reopened on 27 July 1968. This extended the head of navigation to Tyle Mill, eight miles from Reading.

The Transport Act 1968 scheduled this section of the K and A as a cruising waterway. Two other sections also became cruising waterways: from the head of Bull's Lock to the tail of Hamstead Lock (i.e. nearly six miles of waterway through Newbury), and the Avon Navigation. The latter continued to carry commercial traffic until recently.

In 1968 the trust produced a detailed restoration scheme proposing, as a start, restoration of the link from Tyle Mill to Bull's Lock, the section from the River Avon at Bath to Dundas Aqueduct, and of the fifteen-mile pound from Devizes to Wootton Rivers; for a total of £92,450.

To take the items in reverse order, the main work on the fifteen-mile pound was dredging and clearance of rubbish and weed, and some of this has been done, by BWB and volunteers.

At Bath, the principal task was restoration of the flight of seven locks at Widcombe by which the canal climbs away from the Avon. Restoration of the flight was agreed between BWB, K and ACT and Bath City Council in 1969, with the cost to be borne equally by the city council and the trust. The council then made a grant of £7,500 for restoration of the locks and other canal work within the city boundary. This grant, and other grants made subsequently by local authorities elsewhere along the canal, were made to the trust, which has then placed orders with BWB for work to be done. (This arrangement is unique to the Kennet and Avon—elsewhere local authority grants have been made direct to BWB, even for restoration work instigated by voluntary organizations.) Work at Widcombe has been done by BWB staff and by volunteers organized by the local branch of the K and ACT; the lock from the Avon, No. 7, was formally reopened in spring 1970. But it had not seen much use by 1973, to judge from vegetation growing on the cill; though this was not surprising for it gave access only to a few yards of canal with a side pound which awaited development as moorings—the next two locks, in stark contrast, were still derelict, disappearing under weed, their gates sagging and near-rotten. These two locks were due to be replaced by a single very deep lock, as part of a scheme for a new relief road which crossed the canal at the site of lock No. 8 by what would otherwise have been a bridge without headroom for boats. The scheme was planned before 1968, but in 1973 work had not started; it was to be paid for by the DOE as highway authority. Work on the other four locks of the flight appeared complete when I looked at them in August 1973, except for repairs to the masonry of the top lock, while some dredging remained to be done in the intermediate pounds.

The proposal to link the Reading and Newbury cruising waterways has fared worse. The section has several swing bridges which, while adequate for the road traffic of 250 years ago, are less so now. Some were also to carry exceptionally heavy traffic during construction of the nearby M4 motorway. During this period their restoration was deferred, at request of Berkshire County Council, and then deferred again. Also, some of the turf-sided locks were beyond repair, and their reconstruction extremely costly (a 1973 quotation was £35,000 for one lock). Around 1970 the trust's income available for restoration was around £2,500 a year: so it decided, instead of trying to link Reading and Newbury, to propose extension of the Newbury section westwards, along the wholly canal section, where the brick-built locks could be repaired relatively cheaply for £2,000 to £3,000 each. A consortium of local authorities—Newbury Rural District Council, Newbury Borough Council and Hungerford RDC—then provided £4,000 a year for five years to restore the canal from Newbury to Hungerford; Kingsclere and Whitchurch RDC, a nearby authority through the territory of which the canal does not actually pass, granted £1,000 over five years; and the IWA National Waterways Restoration Fund provided £2,500 towards the cost of restoring the first un-usable lock, at Hamstead Marshall. Work started in 1970, princi-pally by BWB staff, and the canal was reopened to Kintbury, two and a half miles and three locks, in May 1972. This had cost £8,500. Kintbury Lock was reopened the following December, and the restorers pressed on towards Hungerford. In August 1973 I noted that work was in progress at Dunn Mill Lock, the last before that town—new top gates had been installed and new bottom gates were awaited. The first boats reached Hungerford on 22 September.

By then another section of the canal had also been reopened, at the east end of the fifteen-mile pound. Restoration of the four locks at Wootton Rivers, giving access from the long pound to the two-mile summit pound, had been envisaged in the 1968 plan for action after its other proposals were complete. The work was brought forward, and the locks were restored in 1971 and 1972 by BWB staff and volunteers from the K and ACT and elsewhere. A formal reopening ceremony was held in June 1973.

Early in 1973, K and ACT plans envisaged restoring the seven and a half miles and nineteen locks between Hungerford and Crofton top lock by 1976: this would link the two main isolated navigable sections to make a continuous length of thirty-seven and a half miles, from east of Newbury to Devizes. It was also intended to restore Bradford-on-Avon Lock (so that supporters at that end of the canal should receive some benefit), and Tyle Mill Lock on the Kennet.

Later that year plans looked like being modified again with developments on the un-navigable Kennet Navigation section. By May the Reading branch of the Trust had, after two years of effort, exceeded its target with a fund for restoring Tyle Mill Lock —£2,380·72 had been raised and the fund remained open to benefit further locks. The next lock above Tyle Mill, at Ufton, raised the water level only a few inches and it was anticipated that it would be possible to do without it. The two subsequent locks, Towney and Padworth, were big problems: turf-sided locks in very poor condition. For their restoration a benefactor made the magnificent offer of £50,000 towards the £72,000 needed, the trust to find the rest. (This may mean a slowing down of work on the Hungerford–Crofton section.) The offer enabled arrangements to be made for work by contract to commence on 1 March 1974; new lock chambers were to be made of steel piling, and the high costs were due in part to remoteness of the sites and difficulties of access by plant. Restoration of these locks will extend navigation for two miles to Aldermaston and the first of the troublesome swing bridges. There was also progress at the opposite end of the un-navigable section: the IWA offered financial help towards reconstruction of Bull's Lock, the first un-navigable lock east of Newbury.

Eventual restoration through from Reading to Devizes would leave two big obstacles to completion on to Bath. The first of these is the flight of twenty-nine locks at Devizes: and of these, the trust has, after considering alternatives such as some form of inclined plane (on which a railway would be laid to carry boats up and down in large tanks of water), declared its intent that they should be restored. The other obstacle is a two-mile section near Avoncliffe Aqueduct which has been kept dry since 1954. By 1973 this section looked to me like a forgotten canal: a depression in the ground covered by turf and bushes. The nature of the ground tends to produce fissures in the canal bed: when the canal was in use it had, on this section, to be repuddled annually. Some years ago the trust carried out extensive but inconclusive experiments to find some alternative way to seal it.

All restoration work on the canal has to be done to specifications and standards approved by British Waterways Board, which as owner and navigation authority has statutory responsibility for the canal in the event of accident or similar occurrence. To maintain and restore the canal, the board employs, under its area engineer at Gloucester, a staff of forty-seven, including two inspectors, about five carpenters and three bricklayers. No more than six or seven men are employed at one time on fitting lock gates. There are maintenance yards at Devizes and Padworth (Aldermaston). Lock gates are made of oak in preference to steel; those installed in restored locks west of the summit have been made at Devizes, and those installed east of it at the board's Worcester depot, squeezed in among River Severn maintenance work.

For voluntary work, to avoid complications the BWB was dealing only with the trust, which organized voluntary work from whatever source it came. As well as helping with restoration, volunteers were helping with maintenance: on the Reading–Tyle Mill and Newbury–Hungerford sections, voluntary lock managers kept locks clean and tidy, mowed grass, applied BWB-supplied paint to gates and grease to paddle gear, planted flower beds and cut towpaths—all to very good effect, from my observations in the Newbury area.

Membership of the trust has grown rapidly during the last few years, in keeping with the increasing pace of restoration. In 1971 it was about 2,500; two years later it was approaching 4,000. The trust was administered by a chairman and a council of seventeen members. In its chairman it was fortunate that the holder of that office, General Sir Hugh Stockwell, was also a member of the British Waterways Board and chairman of the IWAAC. The trust's honorary officials included, in addition to secretary, treasurer etc., an honorary civil engineer. There was one paid employee, a girl to keep the membership records straight.

The trust had in 1973 six area branches: Bath and Bristol, West Wilts (Bradford-on-Avon), Devizes and Pewsey, Hungerford, Newbury and Reading; and two other branches: its Junior Division and the Crofton Society.

The Junior Division was formed in 1965 to encourage young people to participate in the restoration campaign. Its two big achievements—in which it has been aided by volunteers from many local schools, youth clubs, scouts and other youth organizations, were clearance of the west end of the long pound, so that from late in 1965 boats were again able to reach Devizes from Pewsey, after an interval of many years; and removal of overgrowth and general tidying-up around the Devizes flight of locks —which not merely reduces their appearance of dereliction but helps to restrict further deterioration until they are eventually restored. The division has tackled many other similar but lesser jobs; in 1969 it won an award in the Lord Mayor of London's *Venture '69* competition for youth organizations, being placed in the first twelve out of 300 entrants, and the following year it won a 'Countryside in 1970' award.

The Crofton Society restored and maintains Crofton pumping station. This simple statement conceals a venture which could fill a chapter of its own, if not a book. The steam pumps at Crofton are original beam engines of 1812 and 1845: for engines of this type and era still to operate makes them very rare; for them still, at times, to perform their original task (in this instance, raising water from a reservoir to the summit level of the canal) must surely make them unique. The 1812 engine may well be the oldest working steam engine.

In the engine house—and it is a house, arranged with several floors and rooms, its walls supporting the engine components— the visitor is confronted with much up and down movement of rods, at only eleven strokes a minute, massive beams rocking gently high overhead, occasional puffs of steam, and a hooshing of water into the leat feeding the canal—a ton for every stroke of the pump. From engines of this type developed later steam engines and then internal combustion engines such as those in motor-cars and outboard cruisers: Crofton engines seemed to me like grace- fully swaying dinosaurs strayed into an age of small buzzing mammals.

The Crofton engines worked until as recently as 1958; then an electric pump was installed. Ten years later, engines, engine house and surroundings were purchased from the BWB by the trust for a nominal £100 or so, and voluntary restoration began. By 1970 one of the engines was working again, to be joined later by the other. In 1973 the engine house was open to the public every Sunday, with engines in steam during six weekends from April to October. Visitors range from the most erudite to the less-so-but-still-trying ('Ah: the hotwell. They squirt hot water at the steam to cool it. I see.') So great an attraction for visitors has Crofton proved to be that it has become a profitable operation (£1,786 in 1972), and contributes funds for restoration of the canal.

Of similar interest is Claverton pump house, where pumps of the same period are powered not by steam but by a waterwheel. In 1973 they were being restored by engineering students of Bath University; it was planned to open the pump house eventually to the public.

The profit on Crofton was but one of several sources of income for the trust. In addition to subscriptions, donations and local authority support, its money-raising activities included publication of an extensive range of booklets about the canal, proceeds of meetings and boat rallies, sweepstakes and similar operations, and passenger boat operation.

Passenger boats on the separated navigable sections are something of a feature of the K and A, where through-navigation is impossible for any boat too large to portage (though the annual Devizes to Westminster canoe race is famous). The BWB pleasure-boat count for 1972 recorded 572 boats on the canal, without unfortunately detailing either their sizes or the sections on which they were found. Passenger boats were operating in 1973 on the Reading section, from Newbury, on the long pound, and through Bath, most of them at weekends or on Sundays and bank holidays only.

Between Reading, Burghfield and Tyle Mill the vessel used was the *Kennet Water*, privately operated but with bookings arranged through the trust (on commission!). At Newbury was operating the horse-drawn wide boat *Kennet Valley* (horse-drawn, because the owner had the boat, and reckoned attaching a horse easier than installing an engine—and more of an attraction to the public too). She provided an interesting opportunity to see in action the technique of handling tow- and stop-ropes to take the boat past waterside obstructions and through locks—not to mention the chance of observing the tow-rope take up its place in one of those grooves, on the edge of the underside of a bridge arch, which were worn by two centuries or so of passing tow-ropes on canal bridges all over the system but which generally are now no more than reminders of a dead past.

On the long pound, paddle-boat *Charlotte Dundas* was being operated by trust members (and finding a qualified crew regularly must be a problem); another trust-operated boat has sometimes been based on Bradford-on-Avon, but was not running in 1973. At Bath were two passenger boats: a waterbus which started in 1973, run by John Knill, who traded to Newbury in the 1950s; and paddle vessel *Jane Austen*, operated by C. Wray-Bliss, who designed and built her as an enlarged successor to *Charlotte Dundas* which he first operated on this section, and who had a further boat under construction. Myself, wife and dog spent an afternoon on *Jane Austen*, going from Widcombe top lock under the ornamental bridges of Bath and out into the country beyond Bathampton, and back again, sitting on the roof because the passenger accommodation was crowded, in the sun on a hot summer day—and an idyllic experience it was.

The Grand Western Canal

How strange are the inconsistencies in the naming of canals. The title of the Shropshire Union sounds much less impressive than that of its constituent the Birmingham and Liverpool Junction; the original Grand Union was but twenty-five miles of canal through the Northamptonshire countryside; and the Kennet and Avon sounds much less important than the Thames and Severn, although both did link Thames with Severn and of the two canals the K and A was much the most extensive.

So it is no surprise to find that the Grand Western Canal comprises only ten and three-quarter miles of isolated waterway far removed from the main canal system. It did seem to me, though, when in August 1973 I went to have a look at it, a wide canal translated to the Devon countryside of red earth and narrow sunken lanes, that it had been built in the grand manner. With wide and high bridges and an extensive terminal basin at Tiverton, its builders seemed to have catered for large barges such as might have worked on a canal linking the Bristol and English Channels— of which the surviving Grand Western is only a branch, with a short section of main line, of a whole that was never completed. And from the scale of the works it was not difficult to see how building the Tiverton branch had absorbed more money than had been estimated for the whole canal.

The canal was intended to run from Taunton (which already had a navigable link up to the Bristol Channel) to Topsham, on the Exe, with various branches, and was authorized by Act of Parliament in 1796. Because of the Napoleonic Wars, construction did not start until 1809, and then only on the level section from Tiverton to Burlescombe, in anticipation of stone traffic from quarries at the latter place. The canal was eventually extended to Taunton, but not until 1838, and this section had a short life of less than thirty years, while no other part of the canal was built at all. The canal was leased to the GWR in 1854 and later sold to it. On the Tiverton section commercial traffic in stone continued until 1924 and, after serious leakage, a length of half a mile was allowed to dry out, and

75

the canal was split in two, though it remained a statutory navigation until legally closed in 1962.

In 1956 an IWA *Bulletin* reported that Burlescombe parish council had voted in favour of filling in the canal, but that three other councils had voted for retaining it and developing it for amenity. An article in the *Western Times* was quoted as saying that the canal was famous for its water-lilies. A local firm had a contract with British Railways, the owner, to collect them (by boat) and sell them. This appeared to be the canal's main source of income.

By 1961 the corporation of Tiverton considered that the canal should be retained as an amenity. After the canal was transferred at the beginning of 1964 to the British Waterways Board from British Railways (which had latterly been managing it for BWB) rumours were rife that BWB intended to let it dry out. A Grand Western Canal Preservation Committee* was appointed at a joint meeting convened by the Mayor of Tiverton and the chairman of Tiverton RDC; this met representatives of BWB and received assurances that the canal would be maintained as it was.

When an application for planning permission to fill in the canal at Tiverton was made, the committee was reconvened and approved by a well-attended public meeting in Tiverton town hall on 28 September 1966. The committee then negotiated for two years with BWB and obtained an offer to vest the canal in a local authority. The Tiverton councils then appointed the Dartington Amenity Research Trust to report on the future of the canal. The trust recommended that it should be taken over by a local authority and developed as a country park.

A working party was set up of representatives of Tiverton Borough and Rural District Councils, Devon County Council, the Devon River Authority and the preservation committee. Meetings were held between the working party and representatives of the BWB between 1967 and 1969, when negotiations commenced between Devon County Council and BWB to find terms acceptable to both authorities for transfer of the canal to the council.

Provisional agreement was reached in 1970 and the canal was formally handed over to Devon County Council on 5 May 1971. With it the council received £30,000 from BWB towards maintenance and restoration.

The county council's object in taking over the canal was to

* Originally called the Tiverton Canal Preservation Committee.

restore it and bring it into use as a country park. It was estimated that the absolute maximum cost of restoration would be £78,000; it was hoped to reduce this by assistance from the army and voluntary organizations. A canal management body has been set up comprising representatives of the county council, Tiverton Borough and Rural District Councils, and the preservation committee; this was receiving an income of £10,000 a year: £5,000 from the county council and £2,500 each from the two Tiverton councils.

The biggest single work of restoration to be tackled was the dry length. A comprehensive survey and report by the Devon River Authority indicated that the best method of repair, after it had been cleared of nearly fifty years' growth of vegetation, would be to make good the leaks and then line the channel, section by section, with butyl rubber sheet. This work was completed satisfactorily and the dry length refilled during 1973, at a cost of more than £19,000; the work was done by the river authority assisted by the permanent canal staff employed by the county council. A weed-cutting boat has been obtained, and the twenty road bridges across the canal examined and repaired as necessary. Voluntary work has been done by schoolchildren and members of Exeter University.

The management body decided not to permit motor craft, other than those it operated itself. There were in my observation quite a few small privately-owned boats on the canal, and the management body was considering introduction of a waterbus. At Tiverton Basin, which I found pleasantly tidy and (for a town basin) rubbish-free, a hire operator, by agreement with the county council, had punts for hire in 1973: I had half-an-hour's worth (time, if I was to visit the rest of the canal, did not permit a longer cruise), obtaining a punt with oars from a moustached gent in a straw hat, and in this manner, as enjoyable as it was unexpected, navigated a small part of the Grand Western Canal. There were only a few water-lilies, though.

4 · Midlands Waterways

The Wyken Arm

Canals are secretive things, and it is often possible to cross over one by road without seeing it at all. Few travellers passing through the M6 motorway's Spaghetti Junction are likely to be aware that directly beneath the new motorway complex, and invisible from it, is a far older canal crossroads. A little farther to the east, however, motorists on the M6 do catch a brief glimpse of moored craft as they cross over a canal. This is the Wyken Arm (*y* as in *Wye*), off the northern end of the narrow Oxford Canal near Coventry. As often, it is outwardly unremarkable, but it is indeed notable, for it was the first section of disused canal to be restored voluntarily. As long ago as 1959, the arm was reopened after voluntary work organized by the Coventry Canal Society.

Originally the Wyken Arm served collieries, but it seems to have been disused before 1900. By 1958 it was a derelict swamp, useless and offensive. In 1957, however, the Inland Waterways Association had held its national rally of boats at Coventry canal basin, and following that event the Coventry Canal Society was formed; by 1959 it had 300 members. On its committee was David Hutchings, then employed in the city architect's department. He was the prime mover in the restoration of the arm by voluntary labour.

The Wyken Arm was, and is, the property of Coventry City Council, which leased it to the canal society. It is about a quarter of a mile long, and leads to a basin. This was cleared by hand in the summer of 1958 and the spring of the following year. When water was re-admitted from the Oxford Canal it was found that the towpath had subsided, for water flowed over it in seventeen places. It was hastily raised and repuddled. The Oxford Canal at the entrance to the arm was cleared out by steam dredger, and just before the reopening the canal society was loaned a mechanical digger with twelve-foot reach which achieved as much dredging in three days

78

as had been done by hand in as many months. The arm was ceremonially reopened with a procession of thirty boats on 4 July 1959.

When the M6 was built the arm was re-aligned to reduce the
span of the bridge by which motorway crosses canal. In early 1974
there were about sixty boats, belonging to canal society members,
in the basin; at the Oxford Canal end of the arm the Coventry
Cruising Club had excavated a small basin, and with the remainder
of the arm had moorings for a further forty or so boats.

The Stourbridge Canal

It took just two and a half hours to ascend the Stourbridge Canal's
flight of sixteen locks, when I cruised that way in May 1973. There
was little to show that for three epic years, from 1964 to 1967, they
had been the location of the first big joint BWB/volunteer restoration scheme. Only by a couple of badly-leaking top gates, which
might well have been border-line cases for renewal when the canal
was restored, was the canal's condition inferior to that of any other
cruising waterway.

The Stourbridge Canal forms part of a link between, to the west,
the Staffordshire and Worcestershire Canal, Stourport, and the
upper part of the navigable Severn, and, to the east, the canals of
Birmingham and the Black Country. It leaves the Staffs. and
Worcs. at Stourton and for two miles passes through attractive
countryside—remarkably attractive, considering the proximity of
extensive built-up areas. Then an arm goes off to the right to
Stourbridge proper and the through-route starts to ascend the sixteen locks—immediately exchanging rural for urban surroundings.
It passes glassworks for which the area has been noted for two
centuries or more; at the top of the locks, another branch lies
straight ahead while the through-route goes off to the right, to follow the contours to Delph, where it makes an end-on junction with
the Dudley Canal, part of the Birmingham Canal Navigations.
From Stourton to Delph is a little over five miles. Like all canal
approaches to Birmingham, the route has many locks. Between the
Staffs. and Worcs. and the Birmingham level there are twenty-
nine locks—four at Stourton, the sixteen which are at Wordsley,
eight at Delph and one at Blowers Green. All are narrow.

The Stourbridge Canal was authorized by Act of Parliament in

79

1776, on the same day as the Dudley Canal, and opened in 1779. The Company of Proprietors of the Stourbridge Navigation remained independent until nationalization in 1948. Predictably the canal prospered in the canal age, struggled on against railway competition, and was hard hit by the rise of motor road transport in the 1930s. In 1953, an IWA *Bulletin* described it as being in excellent condition, but 'still hardly used at all'.

At the end of 1959 the top lock of the sixteen was padlocked. One of the IWA's oldest, by then, traditions was to voyage through neglected statutory navigations which, it believed, authority hoped to close on grounds of 'no demand': so British Waterways were advised that a boat, which was crewed by prominent IWA members, wished to pass down the locks; and British Waterways responded by suggesting the alternative route via Aldersley (longer by one and a half day's cruising), because a bridge on the sixteen was under repair. In fact, the boat took the short route, and found that some 12 ft. of the canal was obstructed by bricks and masonry, which were removed by volunteers from IWA's Midlands Branch under the direction of David Hutchings (who was later to restore the southern Stratford Canal), but too late for the boat to continue at that time. Following correspondence with the chairman of the British Transport Commission, some seven or eight British Waterways employees were provided to help the boat through at the next attempt. Later in 1960 there were further reports of obstructions in the canal.

In 1962 the IWA decided to hold its national rally at Stourbridge. British Waterways, however, erected notice boards at the sixteen locks to the effect that they were unsuitable for passage of vessels, and all vessels were warned not to attempt to navigate through the locks. British Waterways then invited the Inland Waterways Redevelopment Advisory Committee to approve abandonment of the entire canal—but when the committee paid a visit of inspection it found working boats ascending the sixteen locks!

For the Stourbridge rally, the Wordsley to Stourbridge branch needed to be dredged. The IWA's request to British Waterways to do so, in accordance with the law, produced no satisfactory answer: after taking counsel's opinion, the IWA brought in a dragline and did the dredging itself, with volunteers, two weeks before the rally. And going to and from the rally (at which the total attendance was 118 boats), despite the notices at the locks, forty boats came

7 *Upper* Rows of steel piles are driven into the ground to form the walls of Elsie and Hiram Billington Lock, Upper Avon. The chamber will be excavated from between them. June 1972. (UANT)
Lower Wootton Wawen Aqueduct, Stratford Canal, during restoration in 1962. (David Hutchings)

8 *Upper* A new top gate has been lowered into position at Hazelhurst bottom lock, Caldon Canal. June 1973. (Author)

Lower Buxworth Basin, April 1973. Masonry of gauging lock has been restored, and water is being admitted to the section beyond. (Author)

down the flight and fifty went up, without incident except for removal of debris. Even so, going up or down the locks then became more and more adventurous, with hooligans throwing rubbish in and volunteers clearing it out, and the condition of the locks deteriorating.

At the beginning of 1963 came the replacement, as navigation authority, of the BTC by the British Waterways Board. The new board proved to be much more sympathetic towards the Stourbridge Canal than its predecessor. In June the same year, in preparation for the visit by a small fleet of boats to Stourton village fete, the Staffordshire and Worcestershire Canal Society was given permission to do some voluntary work at the four locks at Stourton. The Society had been formed in 1959, a time when the Staffs. and Worcs. Canal was threatened with closure: its aims were the use and development for all purposes of the Staffordshire and Worcestershire Canal and its adjoining waterways. In 1961 it had offered to British Waterways to provide volunteer working parties for the Stourbridge Canal, and had been turned down.

Discussions between the board and the society took place later in 1963 and in July 1964 the chairman and members of the waterways board held a meeting with the chairman and members of the society's committee. Restoration of the sixteen locks was agreed on the basis that the board would provide capital items, and skilled labour and supervision; the society would provide an unskilled labour force. No prison labour was to be used. A detailed survey of the work needed was made and it is worth studying part of it in full to see just how decrepit a canal can get, for the flight remained navigable, after a fashion, until late in 1964, when a boat was sunk in lock 16 by vandals, and a lock gate was used for Guy Fawkes' night. The list starts like this:

Site and Job	Work to be done by: Society	BWB	Urgency	Remarks
Lock No. 1:				
Top end gate	*	*	1	Replace gate
Top end ground paddles	*	*	1	Overhaul gearing—spares at Stourport
Top end ground paddles	*	*	1	Repair paddles

Site and Job	Work to be done by: Society	BWB	Urgency	Remarks
Lock chamber	*		2	Cut out and rebuild 6 sq. yds. brickwork and point up
Bottom end gate	*	*	1	Replace
Bottom end lock tail	*		2	Slight brickwork repairs
Ponds (*sic*) *1–2:*				
Remove sunken boat	*		1	
Remove sedge growth or spray	*		2	
Clean up towpaths and remove weed growth or spray	*		2 and 3	
Overflow weir	*	*	3	Repairs to weir crest (not urgent)
Overflow weir	*	*	2	Clean out mud bank at weir discharge
Lock 2:				
Ground paddles	*		1	Overhaul gearing
Ground paddles	*		1	Repair paddles
Top end gate	*	*	1	Refit gate
Bottom end gate	*	*	1	Refit gate
Bottom end lock tail	*		2	General pointing to brickwork
Clean off steps	*		2	Replace where necessary
Ponds 2–3:				
Waterway walls	*		1	Brickwork repairs
Remove weed growth or spray with chemical	*		2 and 3	
Overflow weir	*		2	Clean out entrance to weir and remove sedge growth

Site and Job	Work to be done by: Society	Work to be done by: BWB	Urgency	Remarks
Lock 3:				
Paddle gearing	*		1	Overhaul
Paddle gearing	*		1	Repair paddles
Top end gate	*	*	1	Replace
Chamber	*		2	Slight brickwork repairs—pointing
Bottom end gate	*	*	1	Refit
Ponds 3–4:				
Access off main road		*	2	Council to kerb roadside
Towpath	*		2	Make up towpath where scoured out
Debris in canal	*		1	Remove rubbish and clean out accumulated silt
Overflow weir	*		2	Repair weir crest
Overflow weir channel	*		2	Repair damaged brickwork and remove or kill tree roots

and so on, through sixteen locks and five typewritten foolscap pages. Nine new top gates were needed, and three pairs of bottom gates; the total cost was estimated at £7,500.

This, it was intended, would be a pilot scheme for other canals to be restored.

Preliminaries to commencement of work were for BWB to obtain approval of the trades unions to which its employees belonged, and for the society to obtain an insurance policy to indemnify BWB against claims for accidents to volunteers. This type of insurance, then a novelty, was not easy to obtain. Work started in October 1964, at first on clearing undergrowth and trees, and cleaning out lock chambers; repairs to lock gates started in April 1965. General day-to-day liaison with BWB was maintained by D. Tomlinson, the society's vice-chairman. Working parties were held every weekend, with society committee members on a roster to be in charge. A typical Saturday would see four or five volunteers present; a typical Sunday, a dozen. A hard core of fifteen to twenty people came regularly; throughout the whole project perhaps some 200 individuals took part. Notable were excellent relations between the society and BWB staff, particularly the two men regularly employed on the scheme. Volunteers helped to fit lock gates, under their supervision, and there was also a volunteer bricklaying gang. This was reduced at times to using bricks removed from the drained bed of the canal, and when one pound was drained it became clear that the maintenance staff of a canalside factory were in the habit of disposing of faulty bricks by chucking them in the canal. J. A. Robbins, then chairman of the society, recalls how his mock complaint to them that they only threw away the duds resulted, shortly after, in the arrival over the factory wall and on to the towpath of a load of perfectly good bricks!

It had been hoped originally that work would be completed in 1965. But although volunteer support came not only from members of the society (who then numbered about 200) but also from boat clubs, IWA groups and others, work continued into 1966 and it became clear that if volunteers spent the weekend fitting lock gates little else was done. So at the society's suggestion, BWB started to fit gates professionally during the week. Even so, it was 1967 before the flight was again navigable: on 27 May of that year the canal was ceremonially reopened by John Morris M.P., then Parliamentary Secretary to the Minister of Transport.

When the restoration scheme was initiated, it was intended that the canal should be put in order and its situation reviewed after five years to see what use was being made of it. This intention was overtaken by events and the review never made, for by the 1968 Transport Act the main line of the Stourbridge Canal was included in the cruising waterway network. It is now maintained by BWB as part of that network and some lock gates, patched with marine ply during the restoration, have been replaced. An issue of *Navvies Notebook*, published in November 1967, reported that at least 130 boats had used the canal since 27 May, including three Birmingham and Midland Canal Carrying Co. working boats *en route* to Sharpness to load timber.

Map Five   Stourbridge Sixteen and Dudley Tunnel

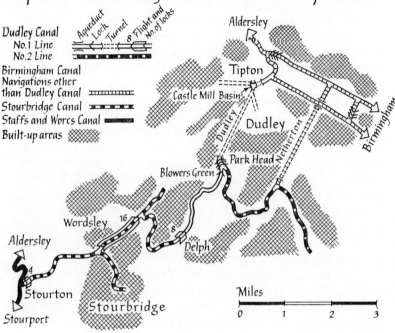

Dudley Canal
  No.1 Line
  No.2 Line

Birmingham Canal
Navigations other
than Dudley Canal

Stourbridge Canal

Staffs and Worcs Canal

Built-up areas

Aldersley

Tipton

Castle Mill Basin

Dudley

Park Head

Netherton

Birmingham

Blowers Green

Wordsley   16

8

Delph

Aldersley

Stourton

Stourbridge

Stourport

Miles

0   1   2   3

Recently, though, I regret to say, the Stourbridge Canal has been seeing less use than many other canals, despite all the effort put into it. The BWB pleasure-boat counts, of boats moving and moored, show the following figures for the years 1967 to 1972: 8, 10, 7, 2, 5, 10; and in the 1972 count, the density of boats per mile was two, compared with an average of nine for canals generally. Of course, too much should not be read into these figures, but they are corroborated by my own experience. A gentleman tending his lock-side garden at Stourton (and to judge from its excellent condition, he must have been spending a lot of his time there) told me about three boats a day were passing—much fewer than on the neighbouring Staffs. and Worcs.—and throughout the Stourbridge Canal, I passed only one other moving boat.

85

Dudley Tunnel and Park Head Locks

Thump. Bang. Crunch of iron boat against ancient brickwork. Paraffin pressure lamps that seemed in the open air no brighter than matches clearly illuminated the wavering bore of Dudley Tunnel, while two open-day boats laden with standing passengers were poled and legged along by members of the Dudley Canal Trust: the first boats to pass through after the tunnel, once abandoned, was officially reopened on 21 April 1973.

Sounds of laughter and snatches of song came out of the darkness, occasional drips of water fell on passengers. 'The calcite formations' said someone through a megaphone 'are formed by particles of lime percolating through the brickwork. Called curtains by the boatmen.' And there they were, like fossil curtains draped along the sides of the tunnel. With no noise of engine or ripples of wash there was little sense of being afloat: just slow, gentle, steady forward motion, as the tunnel walls slipped by, brick by brick by brick.

There is always something improbable about a canal tunnel, with its solid roof and liquid floor: but Dudley is so remarkable that mere improbabilities fade into insignificance. Much of it is indeed ordinary enough, brick-lined, though parts, as a result of subsidence, have very low headroom. But in other places the canal passes through man-made caverns of unlined rock, throws off lengthy branch tunnels, now un-navigable, which formerly served the underground loading basins of coal and limestone mines, and emerges briefly into the open air at a cliff-surrounded pool.

Dudley Tunnel is, I understand, of great interest to geologists, and it is certainly of great interest to historians. With an overall length of 3,172 yards, it is also said to be the longest navigable canal tunnel in Britain, though a purist might point out that its longest continuous section of 2,904 yards is exceeded elsewhere. The tunnel passes beneath the town of Dudley, West Midlands, on the No. 1 line of the Dudley Canal. This connects with the old main line of the Birmingham Canal Navigations (a remainder waterway) at Tipton Junction and runs southwards for four and a half miles to make an end-on connection with the Stourbridge Canal at Delph. By the north portal of the tunnel is the Black Country Museum; at its south end, the tunnel used to emerge into

86

an area of land derelict after 200 years of industrialization. But this, by 1973, was being reclaimed and landscaped, so that on one side grassy slopes led upwards from the canal, while on the other grey and derelict tips reared up, a reminder of what the whole area must have been like. Another reminder was the start of the Pensnett branch, leading out of the Dudley Canal, and solid with sedge and rubbish—the condition to which the Dudley Canal itself was deteriorating a few years ago. The branch left the canal at the top of its three locks at Park Head; below them, the Dudley Canal No. 2 line branches off to the east. From this point on, the No. 1 line becomes a cruising waterway, as part of a through-route from the BCN main line via Netherton Tunnel (opened in 1858 parallel to and a few miles to the east of Dudley Tunnel to relieve congestion among boats using the latter), part of the Dudley Canal No. 2 line and the Stourbridge Canal to the Staffs. and Worcs. Canal and the Severn.

Since Dudley Tunnel itself forms part of a through-route it is unfortunate that few craft will be able to use it, according to arrangements made at the time of reopening. Its headroom is so low as to exclude many boats; and even if they could pass under clearance gauges installed just inside each portal, boats were not, because of limited ventilation, to use their engines. Canoes and rowing boats were also prohibited, so it appeared that boats using the tunnel, which has no towing path, would be limited to cruisers and narrow boats of limited cabin height and of which the crews were prepared to propel them by legging (i.e. by two people who lie, head to head, across the deck and push against tunnel sides with their feet), or by poling against tunnel sides and roof. And even these would only be able to enter at restricted times, southbound in the mornings and northbound in the afternoons, because the tunnel is mostly too narrow for boats to pass one another. So it seemed likely to me that most people who wished to visit the tunnel would do so by public-tripping craft. To my mind, a battery-electric launch would be the ideal vessel; in any event, the Dudley Canal Trust had plans to obtain a powered vessel for round tours including both Dudley and Netherton Tunnels, and in the meantime its open-day boat, working-boat style, was to continue to be manhandled through the tunnel by volunteers to give devotees the full effect.

The oldest part of the tunnel is the northern section: this was

completed in 1778, part of a private canal built by the Lord Dudley
of the time from Tipton to serve his limestone mines; it terminated
at an underground basin, which was later opened out to become
the cliff-encircled pool, Castle Mill Basin. In 1779, the Stourbridge
and Dudley Canals, with which Lord Dudley was also associated,
were open as far as the south side of Dudley. Work started on the
main tunnel in 1785, and the route was open throughout in 1792.
The tunnel became extremely busy, passing as many as 41,000
boats in the year 1853; in the twentieth century traffic declined
and ceased about 1950.

By then the Dudley Canal belonged to the British Transport
Commission, which in 1959 sought powers to close the tunnel and
its approaches to navigation. Despite a protest cruise in October
1960 by the Midlands Branch of the IWA, in which forty boats
participated, the canal from Tipton Junction through the tunnel to
the bottom of Park Head Locks was officially closed to navigation
in 1962. The locks had their paddle gear removed and began to
deteriorate, their chambers silting up, but the tunnel itself
remained in good structural condition. In 1963, however, came a
very real threat when British Railways sought to replace a railway
viaduct over the northern portal with an embankment through
which there would have been a drainage culvert only. Local
enthusiasts started to organize 'last chance' boat trips through the
tunnel, found them popular and formed the Dudley Canal Tunnel
Preservation Society on 1 January 1964. This negotiated with
British Railways with a view to raising the finance needed to
build the culvert large enough for boats. But this was not,
eventually, necessary: following a decline of rail traffic, one of
the railway's two tracks was lifted and the embankment was not
required.

Later in 1964 the Dudley Canal Co. Ltd. was formed, with the
Earl of Dudley having a 51 per cent interest, and the preservation
society, which then had over 300 members, as the second largest
shareholder. This negotiated with British Waterways Board for a
lease of canal and tunnel, but the scheme did not come to fruition.
Meanwhile the preservation society continued its boat trips—
13,000 people were carried by unpowered craft through the tunnel
between 1964 and 1973. But the locks at Park Head deteriorated
until they became impassable, paddle gear or no, and the pound
from the top lock to the tunnel became so silted and rubbish-

strewn that eventually the passenger boat was unable to emerge from the portal.

After the 1968 Transport Act the canal became a remainder waterway; this, and the power the act gave to local authorities to assist financially with waterway restoration, initiated a change in the society's thinking. It enlarged its interest to include the whole of the Dudley Canal, reformed itself as the Dudley Canal Trust, a registered charity, and entered into negotiations with Dudley Borough Council and BWB. It also commenced voluntary working parties on the canal, with BWB approval. Notable was *Dudley Dig and Cruise* of September 1970 when fifty boats and 600 people attended over a weekend. Four feet of mud and debris were removed from one of the lock chambers, pounds between the locks were dredged and masonry repaired.

The trust's efforts were rewarded in January 1972 when Dudley Borough Council agreed to contribute half the cost of restoring the canal, up to a maximum of £4,075, and to accept subsequent responsibility for maintenance up to a value of £500 a year for five years. It later nobly increased its restoration contribution. Overall cost of the scheme was about £18,000; apportionment of this between trust, council and BWB was still being negotiated in November 1973.

New lock gates were fitted by BWB: the rest of the work has been administered by the trust using volunteers, hired plant, friendly contractors and, for repairs to brickwork, Borstal boys. About 20,000 volunteer man-hours went into the project, almost 8,000 tons of mud and debris were dredged from the canal approaches to the tunnel, and even from the tunnel itself 100 tons of mud and rock, which had been washed into the canal from an adjoining mine by a violent storm, had to be removed. In September 1972 the locks were navigated for the first time for ten years; at the end of the year work on the Tipton approach was almost complete and the dredgers moved to Park Head. Six hundred yards of towpath were cleaned, levelled and covered with shale and, after a contractor had let the trust down, volunteers rebuilt a reinforced concrete bridge by the top lock only three weeks before opening day.

The reopening ceremony, entitled *Trad* (*T*unnel *R*eopening *a*t *D*udley) was combined with a rally which attracted about 275 boats. Many members turned out in eighteenth-century costume, cannons were fired and a commemorative plaque unveiled. And since this was the first remainder waterway restoration scheme to be completed in which BWB and a local authority were jointly involved as envisaged by the 1968 act, it was appropriate that while the event was organized by the trust, the actual reopening ceremony was performed jointly by the chairman of BWB and the mayor of Dudley.

The Great Ouse to Bedford

If a prize were to be offered for persistence in the matter of restored waterways, the top award would surely go to the Great Ouse Restoration Society. It was established in 1951 with the aim—by no means over-ambitious—of furthering the restoration of the ten miles or so of derelict navigation over the River Great Ouse, from Tempsford, the then existing head of navigation, up to Bedford. Yet it was twenty-one years before the first lock upstream from Tempsford was restored, and only recently has full restoration of the whole section appeared to be within the society's grasp.

The society did indeed achieve restoration of a lock for the first time as early as 1956, but this was Bedford or Duck Mill Lock, remote from the main navigable part of the river, and its reopening served only to extend slightly an already navigable but isolated and short section through Bedford. Restoration in 1963 of Cardington Lock, the next below Bedford, has so far served even less purpose, for the water level in the reach downstream from it has not been maintained for navigation and this reach has usually been impassable for any but the smallest craft. It was not until 1968 that the decision was taken by the Great Ouse River Authority to build a new lock at Roxton, location of the first derelict lock above Tempsford, and this was opened in 1972. In the meanwhile, in 1969, the GORA had decided in principle on restoration of the rest of the derelict navigation, working upstream, so that restoration of navigation works as Great Barford and Willington was programmed for 1974–5, and it was anticipated that this programme would be taken over by the new Anglia Regional Water Authority which was to supersede the river authority in 1974. This left only one lock, Castle Mills Lock between Willington and Cardington, for which a date for restoration remained to be settled.

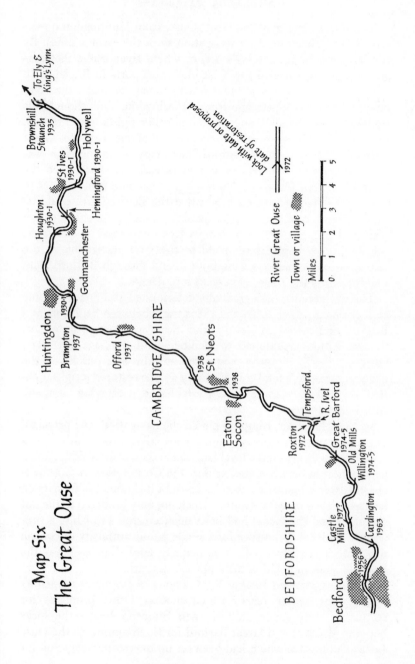

Map Six
The Great Ouse

To Ely &
King's Lynn

Brownshill
Staunch
1935

St Ives
1930-1

Holywell

Houghton
1930-1

Hemingford 1930-1

Godmanchester

Huntingdon

Brampton
1930-1

CAMBRIDGESHIRE

Offord
1937

St. Neots

1938

1938

Eaton
Socon

Tempsford

Roxton
1972

R. Ivel

Great Barford
1974-5

Old Mills

Willington
1974-5

BEDFORDSHIRE

Castle
Mills 1977

Cardington
1963

Bedford

1956

Lock with date of proposed
date of restoration

1972

River Great Ouse

Town or village

Miles

0   1   2   3   4   5

The lower reaches of the Great Ouse, from Huntingdon down-stream, have been used for navigation since the earliest times. By the late middle ages, King's Lynn, where river traffic met sea-going ships, was one of the most important ports in England. In 1617 John Gason was granted letters patent to make the river navigable higher upstream from Huntingdon, and though his rights changed hands many times and other rights were granted, the river had been made navigable by about 1630 to Great Barford, and in 1689 to Bedford. For many years the river was busy with trade, but decline started as early as 1805, when the Grand Junction Canal was built—it passed some twelve miles to the west of Bedford which meant that the Bedford area could be supplied with coal from the Midlands by canal more cheaply than with coal brought by sea to King's Lynn and then up the river. Some improvements were made to the river navigation in the 1840s, but after railways were built to and through Bedford from 1846 onwards the river again went into decline.

The navigation works gradually deteriorated and floods became an increasing problem. By the 1880s trade between St. Neots and Bedford had ceased and local authorities were attempting to have the navigation abandoned to facilitate land drainage. In 1893, however, L. T. Simpson, a wealthy stockbroker, purchased the navigation and at a total cost of some £27,000 restored it right up to Bedford in two years, and also established a carrying company with initial success.

In 1897, however, Simpson closed the navigation. His principal difficulties were that his attempt to get Parliamentary authority to raise tolls to an economic level had met excessive opposition, and a legal action he had initiated against the Corporation of Godman-chester after it had twice exercised a right it claimed, to force open lock gates to release floodwater (which not only hindered traffic but also damaged the locks) had been unsuccessful. Probably, a pre-ference by local authorities for a single public authority to control the river in all aspects (but principally land drainage) was the cause of their opposition to Simpson's activities.

Closure promoted further legal actions in favour of reopening which went on for years without success. Other proposals for reopening were made and in 1906 Simpson leased the locks between Bedford and Great Barford for three months to the Ouse Locks Committee which had been set up to restore navigation for pleasure-craft. Apart from this the locks remained closed, and deteriorated. In 1928 *Bradshaw's Canals and Navigable Rivers of England and Wales* described the river between Bedford and Holywell (thirty-three and a half miles downstream) as 'not now navigable'.

On the land drainage front there was progress. In 1918 the Ouse Drainage Board was set up, and this board, although neither the navigation authority nor the owner of the navigation works, initiated a programme of restoring the locks. Its purpose was two-fold: to enable them to be used as sluices, and so to augment discharge capacities of sluices already existing; and to enable its floating dredgers and plant to be moved up and down the river. During 1930 and 1931 the four locks from St. Ives to Godman-chester were restored and converted. The Great Ouse Catchment Board took over from the drainage board, continued the same policy, and in 1935 purchased the navigation rights. The same year it restored the lock at Brownshill Staunch, below which the river is tidal (although another lock a few miles downstream gives access to further non-tidal Fenland waterways). The catchment board then started to work upstream from Godmanchester, rebuilding the locks at Brampton and Offord in 1937, and St. Neots and Eaton Socon in 1938. These Great Ouse locks are generally longer and narrower than wide canal locks—maximum beam for boats is 10 ft. 6 in. About 1939 the catchment board prepared drawings for schemes at Tempsford, where there was a navigation weir or water gate, and at Roxton Lock; it intended to restore the navigation up to Bedford, and even, possibly, up the long-disused River Ivel, which entered the Ouse at Tempsford.

Unfortunately, the Second World War intervened; the work was not done and, by the time the war was over, dredging techniques had altered: it was now done largely with land-based machinery and transport, so the board had little reason to recommence restoring the navigation works.

No revival of commercial carrying had followed restoration of the locks; but pleasure-craft, particularly motor cruisers, did appear on the river. They passed through the locks without charge, for the navigation rights contained no provision for charging them. At Bedford, too, use of the river for pleasure was of long standing. Even in the early 1700s Celia Fiennes had observed not only that 'this river beares barges' but also that it had 'many little boats . . .

belonging to the people of the town for their diversion'. In more recent times, I have been told, before the motor-car became every-man's symbol of affluence, it seemed that every household had a punt or dinghy on the river. Pleasure trips on the river through the town ran until about 1939, and were revived in 1944 by Silvery Ouse Pleasure Craft, which continued to operate them in 1973.

So discontinuance of the restoration programme caused discontent. In 1950 Bedford Boat Club was formed, and one of its objects was to procure restoration of the Great Ouse to navigation up to Bedford. The then Fenlands Branch of the IWA set up an Upper River Ouse Fighting Fund. On 20 February 1951 the Great Ouse Restoration Society was established at a public meeting at Bedford Town Hall, and took over the campaign.

The society's function has been to agitate for restoration and to reinforce words with cash. It became a registered charity, and appointed trustees to hold its property. Its number of members has varied with progress—up to 200 for the reopening of Bedford Lock in 1956, down to just over 100 in 1962, up to 200 again for the reopening of Cardington Lock and up again to over 400 as the reopening of Roxton Lock approached.

In 1952 it was reported that the chief engineer to the Great Ouse Catchment Board had estimated, after a six-month survey, that £77,000 would be required for complete restoration of navigation from Tempsford to Bedford. At that time this seemed a large sum. The opportunity for practical progress came in 1954 when the Great Ouse River Board (which had taken over from the catchment board) decided to reduce flood risk in Bedford by rebuilding the lock for flood water discharge, with a single guillotine gate at one end. To enable the lock to be used by boats, the restoration society raised £1,250 for a pair of ordinary lock gates to be installed at the other end of the lock. The four miles or so of navigation that resulted had, by 1973, about 150 boats on them, including many motor cruisers.

Cardington Lock was restored on the same basis as Bedford Lock, the society contributing £1,000. Initial clearance work at Cardington was done by volunteer labour, and other voluntary working parties were held by the GORS to clean up and clear out other old lock chambers, particularly at Great Barford and Roxton. They ceased in 1964 when the river board decided that it would be cheaper, when the navigation was restored, to build new locks instead of restoring the old ones. Subsequently there was for many years no voluntary practical work on restoring the Great Ouse: the Great Ouse River Authority advised me in 1972 that although it was not opposed in principle to voluntary work, the works required were major engineering works and beyond the capabilities of any voluntary organization. By 1973, however, there were plans to use voluntary labour to demolish old lock structures on the section remaining to be restored. Much has, of course, been done voluntarily to raise funds.

The Great Ouse River Authority was set up under the Water Resources Act 1963 and its main responsibility was to manage the water resources of the Great Ouse basin, which extends from Oxfordshire to Norfolk. To do this it had to build river-flow gauging stations. In 1968 the location chosen for one of these was just above the confluence of the River Ivel with the Great Ouse— in other words, the site of Roxton Lock and weir.

So a new structure was planned and built at Roxton, including weir, lock and footbridge, which combined the functions of water measurement, land drainage and navigation. Its total cost was estimated at £80,200, allocated thus:

Hydrometric scheme (water measurement) £29,200
Land drainage £29,200
Navigation £21,800

The sum allocated for navigation included not only construction of the new lock but also landing stages, some dredging, and removal of the staunch or navigation weir at Tempsford. Towards it, the GORS was asked how much it could contribute, and suggested £5,000, a far higher sum than it had ever raised before. But the target was met, after four years of raising funds, from, among other sources, boat rallies, raffles, draws, gifts and grants from boat clubs, the Pye Trust and local authorities. Regrettable by its absence from the list of donors was the IWA's National Waterways Restoration Fund. The IWA council, having been advised that the work was to be done entirely by contract and that the cost of the lock was estimated at £35,000 (which figure was clearly either wrong or else subsequently revised), 'regretfully decided' not to make a grant as costs were not being brought to as low a level as possible by use of free labour or by obtaining materials cheaply. Happily the IWA has since relented and contributed from its general funds towards further restoration of the Great Ouse, and when the IWA national rally of boats was held at Ely in 1973, one of its objects was to support restoration to Bedford.

The new Roxton Lock, made of concrete, with steel gates, was opened on 12 August 1972 by the Duke of Bedford. By early 1973 the river had been dredged upstream as far as Great Barford, which became the head of navigation; and the dredger was moved up to Willington, on the un-navigable section, to dredge it principally for land drainage.

In the meantime, others factors had prompted the decision to restore fully navigation from Great Barford to Cardington. The Water Resources Act 1963 gave the GORA powers to make by-laws requiring pleasure-craft to be registered and imposing registration charges on them. This the authority did, and its by-laws relating to boating were made in 1971 (and confirmed not, as on the Lower Avon, by the Secretary of State for the Environment, but by the Minister of Agriculture, Fisheries and Food). This gave it, at last, a source of revenue from pleasure-craft and meant that it was able to view restoration of navigation works much more sympathetically than before. During the year ended 31 March 1973, 3,683 boats were registered with the authority.

Secondly, the river authority had decided in 1969 on a programme of improvements, to reduce floods, to the river over fifty-two miles upstream from Tempsford past Bedford to Newport Pagnell; this scheme resulted partly from the decision to build a new city at Milton Keynes, from the roofs and roads of which it was anticipated that rainwater would find its way quickly into the river. As a result of the programme, the authority decided in principle to restore navigation between Roxton and Cardington. To do so, new locks were needed at Great Barford, Willington and Castle Mills; restoration of the old lock at Old Mills, three-quarters of a mile above Great Barford, could be avoided, and so could the staunch or navigation weir a short distance downstream from Castle Mills.

It is much to be regretted, from the historical point of view, that restoration of navigation on both the Great Ouse and Lower Avon has resulted in destruction of some of the few remaining examples of navigation weirs, although it would scarcely have been practicable to ask present-day pleasure-traffic to accept the extensive delays which their use would involve.

9 Reopening day. *Upper:* 28 May 1973—boats enter the Nottingham Canal side of Great Northern Basin. (E. G. Harrison)

Lower: 21 April 1973—crowds gather at the south portal of Dudley Tunnel to welcome boats carrying the official party. (Author)

10 *Upper* Stratford Canal reopening festival, July 1964. Boats which have come down the canal assembled on the Avon. (A. J. Ross)

Lower Stratford Canal maintenance, February 1973. Volunteers organized by the WRG rebuild the by-pass weir at lock 40. (Author)

In 1972 the GORA and the Water Resources Board sponsored a study of the use of the existing navigation by the Department of Land Economy at Cambridge University, in order to estimate the probable result on the pattern of cruising if the navigation were reopened to Bedford, and to make a cost-benefit analysis. Results suggested that because of congestion among boats on the river at St. Neots, it would be unwise to increase their number until more of the navigation was open towards Bedford.

Immediately Roxton Lock was restored, the GORS started a fund for Great Barford Lock with the aim of reaching £5,000 which it undertook to contribute as its share of the cost. The society has also been asked by the river authority to contribute £5,000 each towards Willington and Castle Mills locks and has promised to try. So its appeal had a new target of £15,000 to cover not only Great Barford but also Willington and Castle Mills locks. The combined fund had reached £5,500 by November 1973.

Most cheering of all, however, was a grant announced at the end of 1972 by Bedford Corporation. The corporation had authorized extraction of gravel from riverside land downstream from the town, and had plans to convert the resulting pits into a marina. It then transpired that this scheme would be self-supporting, and the money earmarked but not required for establishing the marina was to be granted to the river authority for restoring the navigation. The sum was no less than £100,000.

The Welford Arm, Grand Union Canal

In 1957, making a first canal cruise, I travelled along the lovely remote winding summit pound of the Grand Union Canal's Leicester section. It was little used and sedge grew thick along the edges to leave, in many places, a clear channel scarcely broader than the beam of a boat. At the point at which, according to the map, a short branch diverged to the east and the village of Welford, an impenetrable reed-bed blocked the entrance, and the branch itself was invisible beyond it.

Fifteen years later I went that way again, in the summer of 1972. It was pleasant to find that the main canal was busier, the sedge less in evidence, the channel wider; it was pleasanter still to be able to turn into the branch and find it no different in condition from

G   97

the main canal. I passed easily along it and up its single narrow lock to reach, after one and three-quarter miles, the terminal wharf at Welford, where many boats were moored and a hire cruiser business was being established. Between my two visits, the branch had been restored to navigability by British Waterways Board, prompted and assisted by the Old Union Canals Society.

The Welford Arm originated as a navigable feeder to the original Grand Union Canal, which was opened in 1814 from the Grand Junction Canal at Norton Junction to the Leicestershire and Northamptonshire Union Canal at Foxton, and was the last link to be completed in a chain of canals between London and the coalfields of Nottinghamshire and Derbyshire. The old Grand Union was purchased by the Grand Junction Canal Co. in 1893; when in 1929 the Grand Junction in turn amalgamated with the Regent's Canal and many others, the name Grand Union was adopted for the enlarged system.

The little branch to Welford seems to have led an uneventful existence, principally supplying water to the main line, and being used for trade, such as coal, until 1946. Then traffic ceased, it became disused and deteriorated, and the lock became impassable.

In 1964 a band of canal enthusiasts at Market Harborough, Leics., formed the Old Union Canals Society, and proposed restoration of the Welford Arm to British Waterways Board, the property of which it had become. After the Transport Act of 1968 the branch became a remainder waterway. Early in 1968 BWB started work on restoration. This was something of a special case among restoration projects: it was necessary for the arm to be dredged in order to supply water to other canals. Although the lock could have been dispensed with, to restore it meant that it could be used by maintenance craft. The costs of restoration were included in BWB's normal maintenance expenditure.

Volunteers of the OUCS cleared hedges and bushes on both sides of the canal preparatory to its being dredged by dragline by BWB. BWB staff piled 200 yards of bank and restored the lock, removing three to four feet of silt from its chamber, repairing the byweir, installing new cills and gates and installing a new footbridge at its tail. Water was let into the lock without ceremony on 20 June 1968 and it was not for another three days that a motor cruiser arrived and its owner found to his delight that he was the first to use the repaired lock. Much dredging remained to be done

—some 10,000 tons of mud were removed in total—before the arm was restored to full depth. It was formally reopened on 17 May 1969 by Sir Frank Price, chairman of BWB, at a rally of boats which had been organized by the Old Union Canals Society to mark the occasion.

The Caldon Canal

The city of Stoke-on-Trent has for me three notable features. The first of these is the early industrial grot . . . er . . . surroundings which lie alongside the Trent and Mersey Canal through the city— not that these do not have their own fascination: many fine canal-side warehouses deserved better treatment than the dirt and neglect that seemed to be their lot when I cruised that way in June 1973. The second feature is the remarkably attractive countryside which lies immediately to the east: hills which are tentative outliers of the Pennines, wooded valleys of rhododendrons, meadows full of buttercups and black-and-white cattle. The third, for Stoke is a compact place, is the suddenness with which one gives way to the other.

Doubtless Stoke has many other notable features, but these are the three relevant here, for they are the essence of the Caldon Canal or, to be precise, the Caldon branch of the Trent and Mersey Canal. Starting in the thick of the industrial area at Etruria on the summit pound of the T and M main line, and without ever being more than eight miles from the city boundary, it passes through some of the most attractive canal scenery in England.

Or so I have read. At the time of my visit the final eight miles from Hazelhurst to the terminus at Froghall basin, which pass through the Churnet valley and are reputed to be most attractive, were still un-navigable but being restored. The nine miles from Etruria to Hazelhurst Junction were navigable, below standard, and being improved; also navigable after a fashion was the two and three-quarter-mile branch from Hazelhurst in the direction of Leek. This branch is fed with water from Rudyard Reservoir and it and the Hazelhurst to Etruria section serve as navigable feeders to the main line of the T and M—it is to this that they owe their survival.

The approach to the Caldon Canal at Etruria, set in an industrial wasteland with a very sharp bend leading to one still sharper, must have been a discouragement to explorers—though, I found, extensive bank protection works had been done, and had improved it. There followed a staircase pair of locks, where an agile youth was amusing himself and amazing others by leaping to and fro across the seven-feet wide chamber. Further on, the canal passed through Hanley Park, a lesser Regent's Canal along the contour past the bandstand, and continued high on the hillsides, by many more factories including those of a pottery which used the purpose-built boat *Milton Maid*, subsequently joined by *Milton Queen*, for breakage-free inter-factory transport. Then the urban area receded and after Milton the canal, though still within the city boundary, became rural.

The water was clear, the canal narrow and winding, lined by beds of sedge with little more than a boat's width between them. But not everywhere—in places the sedge was conspicuous by its absence, and I passed two dredgers within three miles. Many locks had new gates. Above the flight of five at Stockton Brook the canal was at first broad and straight, then narrow, shallow and obstructed by floating sedge: speed fell to much less than walking pace.

At Hazelhurst Junction the canal was on the southern slopes of a valley; a handsome cast-iron roving bridge spanned the main line to Froghall which immediately descended three locks, while before the bridge the Leek branch diverged round some bushes to the right, and only gained the northern side of the valley, and the direction of Leek, three-quarters of a mile further on where the valley was at its narrowest and the branch crossed over the Froghall line by an aqueduct. Despite the absence of people, for I was there at a weekend, Hazelhurst Locks showed signs of great activity. The first two were restored (though the pounds between the three were still reed-grown, undredged and drained), while work was in progress on the lowest lock. Sheer legs stood over the top end of the chamber, with the new gate just lowered into place. Aground in the empty lock was a motor narrow boat laden with new steel and timber bottom gates to replace the rotten wooden ones still in position. Aground, too, in the reeds in the drained pound above the lock were the narrow boat's butty, laden with materials, and a maintenance punt. Brickwork was freshly pointed, not only on the locks themselves, but also on a lock-side hut.

I was able, a few days later, to visit by road Cheddleton, on the

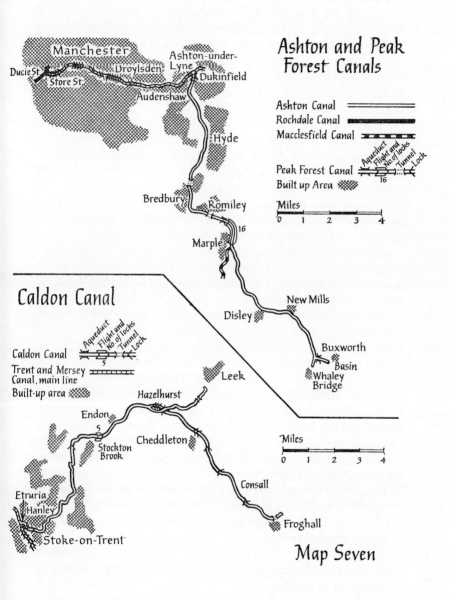

Manchester

Ducie St
Store St.

Droylsden

Audenshaw

Ashton-under-Lyne

Dukinfield

Hyde

Bredbury

Romiley

16

Marple

Disley

New Mills

Buxworth
Basin

Whaley
Bridge

Ashton and Peak
Forest Canals

Ashton Canal
Rochdale Canal
Macclesfield Canal

Aqueduct   Flight and   Tunnel
            No. of locks   Lock

Peak Forest Canal
Built-up Area

                16

Miles
0   1   2   3   4

Caldon Canal

Aqueduct   Flight and   Tunnel
            No. of locks   Lock

Caldon Canal
Trent and Mersey
Canal, main line
Built-up area

                5

Leek

Hazelhurst

Endon
    5
Stockton
Brook

Cheddleton

Consall

Etruria
Hanley

Stoke-on-Trent

Froghall

Miles
0   1   2   3   4

Map Seven

Froghall line, and Froghall itself. At Cheddleton were two locks; the pound above was in water, if weedy; but above the top lock stop planks were in place, and the lock itself was both empty and cleared of rubbish, down to the brickwork of the bottom. The lock chamber's unusual wooden sides had been partly removed to reveal brickwork behind, and the old gates hung loose awaiting replacement. The short pound between the locks was dry, and vegetation suggested it had been so for a long time; but a stack of new steel piles waited, ready for bank protection work. Nearby a notice indicated that a tripping passenger boat would start to run when the canal reopened. At Froghall there was less sign of activity: extensive basins, wharf buildings and skeletons of old boats gradually revealed themselves amid luxuriant undergrowth. But part of the area was being cleared and this, I believe, was work done by Staffordshire County Council, which had purchased the area around the basin as a picnic site.

To revert to Hazelhurst: I navigated up the Leek branch, where the canal followed wooded slopes, until it opened out into a lagoon among the hills. This was my terminus for though the stone portal of a tunnel beckoned onward there is, I understand, nowhere beyond the tunnel for a boat longer than the canal's width to turn, since the basin at Leek has been filled in. Others of the crew navigated the tunnel by dinghy. This spot, remote and not easy of access, was nevertheless busy. First arrived a two-person canoe, and then a narrow boat cruiser, some 60 ft. long. Its steerer, not to be put off by the absence of winding holes, disappeared with his boat into the tunnel going astern. Then came a small cruiser which turned and left immediately, and finally the punt *Flotsam*, crewed by members of the Caldon Canal Society on a driftwood and rubbish clearance expedition. All this took place during an hour or so on a Sunday afternoon.

The Caldon Canal originated from an Act of Parliament of 1776, which authorized the branch from Etruria to Froghall with an extension to limestone quarries at Caldon Low by tramroad—a primitive form of railway on which wagons were pulled by horses. It was opened about 1779 and altered and improved a few years later. The Leek branch was authorized in 1797, and the same year an extension of the Froghall line to Uttoxeter was authorized, and in due course constructed. This lasted only until about 1847, after which it was closed and in part converted into a railway; but a neatly painted milestone at Etruria was still indicating the distance to Uttoxeter in 1973.

The Trent and Mersey Canal passed into railway control in 1845, but the Caldon branch continued to be busy with traffic until within living memory. Then traffic fell away between the wars and in 1944 the London, Midland and Scottish Railway Co., owner of the canal, obtained powers from Parliament to abandon the Leek branch. Happily, except for the final three-quarters of a mile into Leek, this branch remained in existence as a navigable feeder.

The condition of the Caldon Canal must have deteriorated gradually: the extent to and rate at which it did so is now difficult to determine. In November 1960 the hotel boat *Saturn* navigated to both Froghall and the extremity of the Leek branch, and although it was believed to be the largest boat to have made these passages for many years, no great difficulty was reported, except for one bad scour, or silted and shallow section, and some defective paddles. In 1961 British Waterways proposed closure of both the Froghall and Leek lines, which was opposed by local authorities.

About 1961 stop planks were inserted above Hazelhurst top lock's top gate, which was said to be unsafe, and the Hazelhurst to Froghall section became inaccessible. From then until 1968, when the Transport Act rendered the whole Caldon Canal a remainder waterway, the Gilbertian situation existed that the Froghall line, though a statutory navigation, was inaccessible, while most of the Leek line was still navigable, more or less, though statutorily abandoned. About 1963, 150 feet of the Froghall line near Consall was piped, as its bank was in danger of slipping on to an adjoining railway line. The same year it was stated in an IWA *Bulletin* that negotiations were in progress for transfer of the whole branch to the National Trust; evidently these were unsuccessful.

Local concern about the fate of the canal was increasing, however; and after a public meeting at Leek on 18 February 1963 the Caldon Canal Committee was formed—a committee open to everyone interested rather than limited to paid-up members (this, it was presumably considered, would be easier to dissolve in event of failure!). That spring BWB gave permission for the cast-iron roving bridge by which the towpath of the Leek line crossed the Froghall line at Hazelhurst to be painted voluntarily. In 1965 BWB authorized towpath clearance by volunteers and by 1966 eight miles of hedges had been cut back. Stoke-on-Trent Boat Club provided the backbone of the volunteer working parties, but many other voluntary organizations were represented. Voluntary work has continued ever since—mainly agricultural, it has included, in addition to hedge-cutting, removal of silt from lock chambers, weed from the channel and rubbish from both. In 1967 BWB had a dredger at work between Etruria and Hazelhurst, and in 1969 installed some new gates in locks on the Stockton Brook flight. In 1971 the IWA loaned £1,250 to BWB for further repairs to these locks so that its North-western Area could hold its annual rally of boats at Endon, between Stockton Brook and Hazelhurst.

Meanwhile the Caldon Canal Committee had been negotiating for full restoration with both BWB and local authorities; the better to be able to negotiate with the latter, it had transformed itself into the properly constituted Caldon Canal Society. This, it says, exists to restore, preserve and maintain in good order the Caldon Canal.

Early in 1971 it was stated in an IWA *Bulletin* that BWB agreed on principle to restoration, but required the backing of local authorities. This was forthcoming late in the same year when agreement was reached between BWB, Stoke-on-Trent Corporation and Staffordshire County Council for restoration of the canal from Etruria to Froghall, with the local authorities contributing to costs of restoration and future maintenance. Work started in August 1972—the BWB chairman ceremonially lowered a new lock gate into position—and was due to be completed by April 1974. The estimated cost of the scheme was about £85,000, of which the BWB was to contribute £35,000, the equivalent of dealing with the canal in the most economical manner in accordance with the Transport Act 1968. In addition to lock repairs and dredging, big jobs were the bank protection and anti-subsidence work I noted close to the junction at Etruria, the removal of the piped section near Consall and its replacement by a concrete channel some 100 yds. long, 10 ft. wide and 4 ft. deep—this was done by contract in 1972—and repairs to the brickwork of the short tunnel by which the canal approaches Froghall basin.

Volunteers organized by the canal society were doing much more work on the towpath, to make it walkable from end to end as part of the restoration scheme. Towpath grass was cut with an Allen mechanical scythe, transported from site to site on a trailer. To overhaul this trailer took up one person's spare time for six weeks in 1973, which is a good example of the sort of behind-the-scenes work involved in voluntary waterway restoration. Volunteers also did much preliminary work on the canal itself, such as clearance of bridge holes and lock chambers. Most of the rest of the work was being done by BWB employees. During the spring of 1973—a typical period—eleven BWB men were employed full-time on restoration work: six of them dredging, one bricklaying, one carpenter and six labourers. These were supervised by a foreman and a section inspector, who also had responsibilities on the Trent and Mersey main line. Indeed to restore the Caldon within the time limit (imposed as a result of impending reorganization of local government) meant taking men and equipment off the maintenance of the main line. New lock gates needed were made by BWB at its Northwich yard; and, at the time of my visit, as I have indicated, the whole scheme was in full swing.

5 · Pennine Chain

The Ashton and lower Peak Forest Canals

Had you wished, around 1835, to send a parcel or a consignment of goods from Manchester to Nottingham or thereabouts, it would probably have taken a route which today seems most improbable.

From Manchester it would have gone by narrow boat, up the Ashton Canal to Dukinfield and then up the Peak Forest Canal to Whaley Bridge in the Peak District. There the boat would have floated straight into a handsome warehouse in which the waterway was matched on either side by railway lines, and the parcel would have been transferred to a wagon of the Cromford and High Peak Railway, which continued the route direct from the far end of the warehouse. This early railway was laid out in a manner not unlike a canal—long level sections, on which wagons were pulled by horses, interspersed with steep inclines, corresponding to flights of locks, up or down which wagons were raised or lowered by cables. In this manner the parcel would have been hoisted over the southern Pennines, by a route too rugged for a canal, and deposited at the railway's far terminus alongside the Cromford Canal near Cromford. There, it would have been transferred back to a canal boat, to travel down the Cromford Canal as far as Langley Mill, and thence over the Nottingham Canal to Nottingham.

This combination of rail and canal did not last long as a through route. The railway, after becoming for many years part of the main railway system, is now closed—although the warehouse at Whaley Bridge still survived in 1973, despite proposals to demolish it, and was surely an almost unique survival of that brief era when railways, though fast developing, still co-operated with canals rather than competed with them. Of the canals, some were abandoned and few were, in 1973, navigable. What is remarkable—and also accounts for this lengthy digression into transport history—is that in 1973 there were, along or close to this route, no less than four separate canal restoration schemes; and in addition one of the large stationary steam-engines which worked an incline (Middleton Top) on the railway had survived to become an ancient monument.

The canal restoration schemes were those for the Ashton and lower Peak Forest Canals, for Buxworth Basin, for the Cromford Canal from Cromford to Ambergate, and for Great Northern Basin at Langley Mill. Of these, the most extensive was that for the Ashton and lower Peak Forest Canals.

Both the Ashton and the Peak Forest canals were promoted in the 1790s and opened within a few years. The Ashton Canal runs from a junction with the Rochdale Canal at Ducie Street in central Manchester eastwards by Droylsden and Audenshaw for eighteen narrow locks and a little over six miles to Ashton-under-Lyne. Branches once more than doubled the total mileage but are all now statutorily closed, as is the Huddersfield Narrow Canal with which the Ashton Canal connected at Ashton itself. The Peak Forest Canal leaves the Ashton Canal at Dukinfield, six and a quarter miles from Ducie Street, and runs in a generally south-easterly direction for nearly fifteen miles to Buxworth, via Hyde, Romiley, Marple and New Mills; from a junction three-quarters of a mile short of Buxworth, a half-mile branch leads to Whaley Bridge. This south-eastern end of the canal passes through a region of deep valleys among high moorland—ambitious country to build a canal through, and the summit pound is now, at 518 ft. above sea-level, the highest pound on the cruising waterway system. To reach it the canal had sixteen narrow and deep locks, all in one imposing flight at Marple. The lower part of the flight is set in pleasant sylvan surroundings, and near its foot is an impressively high stone aqueduct over the River Goyt.

The importance of the Peak Forest Canal was enhanced when it became part of two through routes to Manchester: from the Nottingham area via the C and HPR, completed in 1831, and from the Birmingham area via the Macclesfield Canal, opened the same year. This canal runs from a junction with the Trent and Mersey Canal near the Potteries to join the Peak Forest Canal above Marple top lock.

Traffic on the three canals was once heavy, as is confirmed by the many canalside mills and warehouses which survive, and, in Manchester, by the remains of numerous wharves and private branch canals. In 1838, tonnage carried on the Ashton Canal was

514,241. Heavy traffic continued after the canals came under railway control in the 1840s for they enabled the owning railway company—it eventually became the Great Central Railway—to extract business from districts served by railways of competing companies but not by its own.

Between the First and Second World Wars, traffic fell away, and ceased on the Ashton and Peak Forest Canals in 1954 when a mill which had received coal over them was destroyed by fire. By then the Ashton, Peak Forest and Macclesfield Canals were all part of the nationalized network. In 1953 a note in an IWA *Bulletin* about the Ashton Canal reported little fundamentally wrong, though there was much junk in it, particularly at swing bridges—its trouble was lack of traffic. Some pleasure traffic did remain, though by 1959 the Ashton Canal was excluded from navigations covered by the general British Waterways cruising licence.

The last occasions, prior to restoration, when the lower Peak Forest and Ashton Canals were navigated from Marple to Manchester were in the spring and summer of 1961. By then, Marple Locks had deteriorated badly. A notice at the top lock warned that they were 'not recommended for pleasure-boating' and boats that did pass down encountered rubbish-strewn locks, rotting lock gates and paddles that carried away with water pressure. But the Ashton Canal, which runs through an entirely industrial area, was far worse. Its near-derelict locks were obstructed by every form of junk from bricks to bus seats; the crew of one of the last boats to pass through found the bottom gates of one of the locks just destroyed, burned by vandals, their remains still warm. Not to be beaten, they *carried* their 17 ft. cruiser round the lock; the fourteen and a quarter miles journey from Marple to Manchester took them three days.

Shortly after this the waterway across the Ashton Canal's aqueduct over Store Street, Manchester, was replaced by a pipe to prevent leakage and the section became impassable, though not legally closed.

The Macclesfield Canal and the upper Peak Forest Canal (from Marple to Whaley Bridge) continued to be used by pleasure-craft and survived to be graded as cruising waterways by the 1968 Transport Act. The Ashton and lower Peak Forest Canals, and the short section of the Peak Forest leading to Buxworth Basin, became remainder waterways; the story of Buxworth Basin is recounted later in this chapter.

Over the lower Peak Forest and Ashton Canals, meanwhile, there had been raging a controversy probably more acute than over any other un-navigable waterway for which full restoration has since been agreed. Their significance for pleasure cruising was that they formed a missing link of fourteen miles in the ninety-eight miles Cheshire Ring formed by the Ashton, lower Peak Forest and Macclesfield Canals, and parts of the Trent and Mersey, Bridgewater and Rochdale Canals. The short section of the Rochdale Canal involved is worthy of note: one and one-eighth miles long, with nine wide locks, in central Manchester, it is the only surviving section of that canal which has not been statutorily closed to navigation and has been maintained by the independent Rochdale Canal Co., with voluntary assistance, to give access to the Ashton Canal. In 1973, impending reopening of the Ashton and lower Peak Forest Canals prompted a programme of improvements, including renewal of many lock gates.

Back around 1961, however, when the Ashton Canal was still just navigable, a conference of local authorities, including Manchester Corporation, had recommended its closure. Fifteen children had drowned in the canal in the previous eighteen years. (The subject of canals in which children drown is a distressing one, into which I do not intend to digress here, apart from pointing out that many human enterprises and activities involve an element of risk to children but are none the less accepted without question.) Later in 1961, 400 people crammed a public meeting, chaired by the managing director of *The Guardian* newspaper, and passed *nem. con.* a resolution, for delivery to the Minister of Transport and others, calling for restoration of the Ashton Canal in accordance with the the law and its fullest use for trade and amenity.

But the Ashton and lower Peak Forest Canals continued to deteriorate. No effort appeared to be made to keep Marple Locks clear of obstruction, and hooligans had a clear run. Early in 1962 came a disaster, when part of the side of Marple Aqueduct collapsed. The whole canal was closed for repairs and water piped across the aqueduct. Then a local authority came to the rescue: at the instigation of the Urban District Council of Bredbury and Romiley, which was concerned at the break in the canal link, the aqueduct was scheduled as an ancient monument. This enabled Cheshire County Council to contribute towards its full repair, done in 1964.

At this period, the National Trust was restoring the southern Stratford Canal, and a similar scheme was considered for the lower Peak Forest, without result.

In 1964, however, the Peak Forest Canal Society was founded. Its objects were, according to its literature, to promote and maintain the amenity value of the Cheshire Ring canals by conservation of scenic features and ensuring their continuance as part of an integrated system of navigable waterways. In 1969 it was incorporated as a guarantee company, which is also a registered charity. Membership, 143 in January 1965, was about 700 by April 1973, with 132 new members enrolled during the previous six months. To make its views known and promote restoration of the Ashton and lower Peak Forest Canals, the PFCS has held public meetings, exhibitions and film shows. It has organized visits by local authority representatives to improved canals in other areas such as Birmingham. It has consulted and co-operated with other organizations such as angling and boat clubs. It has produced publications —in 1970, for instance, 25,000 copies of a well-produced leaflet, a joint publication with the IWA, which contrasted what Birmingham was doing to improve its canals with what Manchester was not, were distributed among councillors, aldermen, churches, chapels and all premises, both residential and industrial, within a quarter of a mile of the Ashton Canal.

But most important have been working parties organized by the society, attended both by its own members and by visiting groups. In 1965 the PFCS was authorized by BWB to do agricultural work along the canals, intended as clearance of sedge and tidying of towpaths; though the society somehow extended the definition of *agricultural* to include replacement of three rotten lock gate balance beams. The new beams, made from suitable second-hand timber, cost £15: against an official estimate, according to *Navvies Notebook*, of £300. Later, by agreement with BWB the society was able to repair paddles and start clearance of lock chambers.

In 1965 also, *The Facts About The Waterways* showed that, with the very limited maintenance they were receiving, and much revenue from sale of water to industry, the Ashton and lower Peak Forest Canals sometimes produced a surplus of revenue during a year; though if made into tidy water channels, or eliminated, they would have been in deficit.

In 1966 the IWA held its annual national rally of boats at Marple, in support of restoration of the un-navigable canals. This attracted a record attendance of 212 boats with a further thirty-eight at a subsidiary rally on the Rochdale Canal in Manchester. At Marple, small craft were launched at the bottom of the locks and cruised to Romiley. Boat rallies at Marple then became a regular occurrence, and in 1971 another rally on the Rochdale in Manchester was attended by 100 boats.

On 24 January 1968, the Attorney-General, at the request of thirty plaintiffs which included the IWA, the PFCS and eighteen local authorities, issued a writ on the British Waterways Board alleging that it had failed to carry out its statutory duty to maintain the Ashton and lower Peak Forest Canals. Preparations for this legal action had been going on since 1965 and had been completed late in November 1967; then on 8 December was published the Transport Bill containing proposals to repeal the law on which the action was based. The plaintiffs decided to go ahead, for the provisions in the bill might not have been passed.

To disentangle the events of the rest of 1968, I find it easiest to tabulate them:

28 June. Aware of the government's difficulties, the plaintiffs' solicitors write to the Minister of Transport suggesting that he should either include the two canals in the proposed cruising waterway network or enable the plaintiffs to take them over.

5 July. Letter acknowledged.

25 July. Lord Chancellor alleges in House of Lords that the legal action was whipped up to spike the Transport Bill. Allegation subquently withdrawn.

19 September. BWB invites local authorities along the canals to a meeting to be held on 16 October.

21–2 September. *Operation Ashton.* After three months of planning, some 600 volunteers from many parts of Britain clear 2,000 tons of rubbish from the Ashton Canal during a weekend of pouring rain, as a demonstration of what could be achieved. The largest working party on canals to date, it cost the organizers £1,300, all met by voluntary donations; £750 was spent on plant hire.

4 October (Friday). Ministry of Transport denies knowledge of plaintiffs' letter of 28 June.

7 October (Monday). IWA assists Ministry to find letter by quoting Ministry reference number.

8 October. House of Lords, debating Transport Bill, decides by a small majority that legal proceedings against BWB should continue.

9 October. Plaintiffs make offer to BWB to settle, conditional on Lords' amendment staying in bill. The proposal is that plaintiffs form a consortium to take over the two canals: BWB to participate if it wishes. It is suggested BWB pays £70,000 to consortium, estimated as representing its inescapable minimum costs in relation to the two canals; plaintiffs to find additional finance to restore them.

16 October. BWB chairman and other representatives meet representatives of riparian local authorities in Manchester. All local authorities welcome prospect of resolving the uncertainties regarding the two canals; those along the Ashton mostly favour closure, but those on the Peak Forest are strongly in favour of retention and improvement. This meeting caused much resentment at the time among those plaintiffs in the legal action which were excluded from it.

21 October. House of Commons debate on Transport Bill. Government motion rejecting Lords' amendment carried by small majority. This has the effect that the legal proceedings can proceed no further.

Early in 1969 the BWB had more discussions with the local authorities. These led to establishment of joint BWB/local authority working parties—i.e., study groups—one for each canal, with technical sub-committees; and these considered the possible courses of action and their financial implications. In March the BWB chairman, with some of his staff, met the IWA chairman and some of its council members to discuss the two canals.

The next two and a half years were occupied by attempts, with gradually increasing success, by the pro-canal faction to convince councillors of the desirability of restoring the Ashton Canal; and by detail discussions of the probable costs, of restoration or otherwise, of both canals. (Estimates for restoring the Ashton ranged from £41,000 estimated by the IWA in 1968 to £195,000 mentioned by

11 The Stratford in summer: near Wootton Wawen. May 1973. (Author)

12 *Upper* Pleasure-craft moored at Evesham, Lower Avon. July 1973. (Author)

Lower Pleasure-craft moored at Pewsey Wharf, Kennet and Avon Canal. August 1973. (Author)

the government in the House of Lords.) In June 1970 the IWAAC recommended restoration of the Ashton Canal, and in September the same year the lower Peak Forest study group agreed to recommend to its local authorities that the canal be restored to cruising standards. A joint steering committee was set up for both canals.

As a result of its deliberations, late in 1971 the respective local authorities agreed in principle to restoration of both canals to cruising standards and to contribute much of the cost. It was decided that work should start in April 1972, with the aim to complete by 1974.

Total cost of restoration was estimated at £225,000, that is £179,000 for the Ashton and £46,000 for the lower Peak Forest. Local authorities were to contribute a total of £86,000, including £44,303 from Manchester and £12,000 from Cheshire County Council. Other contributing local authorities were those for Lancashire, Droylsden, Audenshaw, Ashton-under-Lyne, Dukinfield, Hyde, Bredbury and Romiley, and Marple. The IWA had offered £10,000, from the National Waterways Restoration Fund, and the PFCS agreed to contribute £3,000. British Waterways Board was to provide £126,000, its estimate of the minimum cost which it would incur whatever happened to the canal. News of agreement to restore a canal is always welcome, but I cannot help reflecting that the BWB would have done better had the House of Commons not rejected the House of Lords amendment in 1968— in which event the board would have been able to settle, if so minded, for £70,000. A BWB estimate for filling in and piping the Ashton Canal had been reported by the IWA in 1970 as being over £400,000, and for water-channelling reputedly £90,000. Comparable figures for the lower Peak Forest were £458,000 and £30,000. It is also relevant to note, as a comparison, that to convert two and a half miles of the closed Rochdale Canal in Manchester into a shallow water channel has cost £450,000.

During the years of negotiation voluntary work had been increasing on the two canals. But for the start of the official restoration programme, an event surpassing even *Operation Ashton* was organized on 25 and 26 March 1972 by the Waterway Recovery Group in co-operation with BWB. This was *Ashtac*, Ashton Attack, and has still not been exceeded in size by any other voluntary working party on inland waterways at the time of writing. The principal object was to remove rubbish from the canals in the region of Dukinfield, to enable BWB's waterborne dredgers to follow. It would be an impertinence for me to attempt to describe this event, not having, to my regret, been present: so I shall fall back on statistics, published afterwards in *Navvies*, which give its flavour:

There were present:
804 volunteers who booked in
150-plus who did not
and
3 Hy-mac 580c hydraulic excavators
3 JCB 3c loader/excavators
2 Smalley 360/5 hydraulic diggers
2 8-ton jib cranes
2 12-ton hydraulic cranes
18 tipping trucks
1 Jones KL5 mobile crane
9 dumpers from 15 cwt. to 2 tons
$\frac{1}{2}$ mile of monorail track and 6 trucks
The volunteers consumed (*inter alia*):
3,000 cups of tea and coffee
185 pints of milk
2,000 paper cups
10 lb. tea
2 lb. coffee
50 lb. sugar
6 gal. concentrated orange drink
56 lb. broken biscuits

This time 3,000 tons of junk were removed from the canal, and BWB engineers estimated the value of the work at between £15,000 and £20,000. The cost to the organizers was £1,800, of which £1,000 was provided by BWB.

The full programme of restoration for both canals then got under way, with the Peak Forest Canal Society organizing the voluntary aspect. It appointed four voluntary working party organizers, two for each canal; and every two months, for each canal the appropriate working party organizers met the appropriate BWB area engineer and his deputy, to review progress and plans.

Groups of volunteers from many other organizations came to

help: their organizers liaised with the PFCS working party organizers. On the Ashton Canal, work needed included renewal of gates at seventeen of the eighteen locks, piling the banks along a length which had suffered colliery subsidence, much dredging and restoration of Store Street Aqueduct. The latter, agleam with fresh mortar, was again full of water when I looked at it in April 1973. All plant was being provided by BWB, and its employees were working at weekends alongside volunteers. On the lower Peak Forest the bulk of the work was at Marple Locks, with dredging and renovation of swing bridges elsewhere. On this canal, voluntary working parties tended to work separately from BWB staff, at weekends, and were authorized to control the water-levels themselves. Plant was hired by the PFCS, with BWB reimbursing some of the cost.

At Marple Locks the plan was to start at the top, renewing gates professionally on weekdays and clearing lock chambers by voluntary labour at weekends. Then, after water had been readmitted, the intervening pounds could be dredged by floating dredger. By the time I visited the canal in April 1973, voluntary clearance had reached lock nine, about half-way down the flight. The PFCS's techniques had developed since its early days when locks were cleared by loading silt and rubbish into an oil-drum to be hoisted by hand. To clear lock nine, thirteen volunteers were at work. Eight of them, clad in waders and safety helmets, were wallowing at the bottom of the lock chamber, loading mud and junk into two one-ton capacity skips. These were hoisted and lowered alternately by a crane, hired with operator. The other five volunteers were at the surface: two driving hired dumper trucks, two loading them and one controlling traffic as the dumpers went to and fro across a main road. In this way the PFCS had found that it could clear the contents of a lock chamber—usually 100 tons or so—in a weekend. In my observation (from both top and bottom of the lock chamber) the rate of work was such that the crane was constantly in use; and rubbish found among the mud in the lock in the course of an hour or so included a small bicycle, pieces of paddle gearing, bricks, stones, timber, steel rods, drain-pipes both broken and whole, and a toy submarine. But this sort of haul would have seemed small beer to veterans of Operation Ashton who found several unexploded bombs and the wheels of a post-chaise; or of another lock on the Marple flight, which was found to contain most of the equipment of a forge which had stood nearby—including bellows and anvil!

As well as practical voluntary work, the PFCS was busy raising funds for restoration from sources such as sponsored walks and coffee evenings. Its campaign stall attended boat rallies stocked with sales goods such as T-shirts emblazoned with mottos from *Go to work on a canal* to *I have canal knowledge*. The society was also approaching canalside industries for assistance on grounds of environmental improvement.

At the end of March 1973, Bredbury and Romiley UDC was already advertising a site for a marina adjoining the canal near Romiley. Having contributed much to the restoration campaign, that council certainly deserved, in my oninion, to see some of its money back.

Less happy news was the plan for a motorway by-pass at Hyde, which involved diverting the canal and de-watering a section for about nine months in 1974. Otherwise, restoration of the two canals looked like being completed on time in April 1974, before you read this. By then, the PFCS anticipated, it would be helping BWB with voluntary maintenance.

Buxworth Basin

Buxworth Basin, when I visited it early in April, 1973, proved to be a fascinating place. Not that its fascination was revealed instantly, or all at once: the car bumped to a standstill over a rough lane beside a largish basin, partly full, from which temporary dams prevented water entering two overgrown arms. But this piece of water, though eighty feet wide, turned out to be only the entrance basin: a scramble through the undergrowth showed that the two 'arms' led to a further complex of half-dry basins and disintegrating quays. Where once were warehouses, limekilns and a dry dock was now a wilderness of sedge and willows, long grass and bushes. Past it I had driven down the lane, which proved to be the towpath, without comprehension.

Beyond the entrance basin were a gauging lock and several hundred yards of approach canal, all clear, in water and, again, seemingly innocent of drama, but in fact the outcome of several years' painstaking work by the Inland Waterways Protection

Society to recover them from as derelict a state as the rest of the basin.

The whole area is the original upper terminus of the Peak Forest Canal (the line to Whaley Bridge being a branch) and at Buxworth the extensive basin was laid out for exchange of traffic, particularly stone, with the Peak Forest Tramway. This, a primitive railway on which wagons were drawn by horses, was built at the same period as the canal and extended its route, up gradients too steep for a canal, to quarries at Doveholes near Chapel en le Frith.

In its day Buxworth, or Bugsworth as it was formerly called, was described as a thriving inland port, its basins holding more than twenty boats and its stables more than forty horses for them. The tramway survived unmodernized into this century but was disused by 1926; the basin probably became disused about the same time. Stop planks were put in some 500 yards down the canal and the basin drained of much of its water. It then seems to have been more or less forgotten, though there remained a statutory right of navigation over it until the 1968 Transport Act. In the mid-1950s the IWA noted that the basin was unsightly and malodorous and that local parish councils wanted it filled in; it suggested that the BTC should comply with its obligation to keep the basin in good order, and proposed its development as a marina (and also found it necessary to explain what a marina was, that ugly word not then being in general use this side of the Atlantic). There was no result.

About 1960 the basin and its derelict condition came to the notice of the Inland Waterways Protection Society, which campaigns for the restoration, preservation and development of the inland waterways of Great Britain. At that time the society was making a detailed survey of the Peak Forest, Ashton and Macclesfield Canals in order to oppose (with eventual success) their intended closure. The society then proposed restoration of the basin, and eventually in 1968 reached agreement for this with the British Waterways Board.

This agreement was for the society to restore the basin on a wholly voluntary basis: the BWB could supply neither labour nor equipment. It was, however, able to offer 600 tons of puddling clay, worth about £750, for delivery as and when needed. An estimate, obtained by the IWPS, of the cost of restoring the basin by contract was about £40,000.

Restoration, at Buxworth, has been taken more literally than on other canals. The waterway is being slowly and painstakingly restored to its original condition. The society was, for instance, determined to restore the canal to its full original depth, and was not deterred by the discovery that, because this section was regarded as a reservoir, its original depth had been 5 ft. 6 in., deep for a narrow canal. The stone wall alongside the towpath, too, has been repaired in stone, not concrete—and often with original stones recovered from the canal bed.

In September 1968 work started, from the stop planks inserted in the approach canal. From there to the far end of the basin lay some 1,100 yards of derelict waterway. The first section of 100 yards was tackled first; here, the canal runs along the foot of a wooded hillside, and, during the years of dereliction, the wood had spread across the canal. From the section were extracted no less than 100 mature trees, and the holes left by their roots were filled with clay puddle. There were also found to be three bad leaks in the canal bed, one of them a fissure fifteen feet deep, which had to be filled and sealed. There was a layer of dense sedge to be removed, much near-solid silt to be hoisted out and tipped elsewhere, and the whole channel carefully cleaned out down to the original width and depth. Equipment used included a crane, dumper trucks, pumps, sheerlegs, wheelbarrows, etc., and all had to be carefully maintained. A clay dam was built at the end of the first section and on 3 August 1969 water was admitted, probably for the first time in forty years or so. The forest had been transformed back into an attractive length of canal, and for this work the society gained a Countryside Award in 1970, European Conservation Year.

Work continued on the same basis and water was admitted to the next section, of 120 yards in 1970; and by the time of my April 1973 visit some 500 yards of canal had been restored, together with the masonry of the gauging lock, in which boats used to be gauged to determine their loads and so the tolls payable; and water was even then being allowed to trickle slowly into the entrance basin, slowly so that any leaks might be detected as the basin filled.

The stop planks in the approach canal were still present, however, and Buxworth Basin was not yet accessible to boats. Nevertheless, the society was approaching completion of the first phase of its restoration project, undertaken, in the words of Mrs. B.

Bunker, honorary secretary of the IWPS, 'for the good of the country'.

The Cromford Canal (Cromford to Ambergate Section)

Heavy and unseasonable snow had produced alpine conditions overnight, encrusting branches of trees, flattening daffodils and covering hills all round with whiteness that glistened in bright sunshine. When I set out to walk alongside the disused Cromford Canal in April 1973 it was with two inches of snow on the towpath. Cromford is in Derbyshire, in the valley of the River Derwent, surrounded by highish hills; the Cromford Canal commences at a pleasant roadside wharf with a group of canal buildings including a warehouse from which the awning still projected over the canal to shelter imaginary boats. Part of the wharf was used as a coal yard, though coal was last delivered by water, I understand, in 1937.

The canal appeared shallow and was overhung by bushes and trees; there were occasional signs of agricultural clearance work. At High Peak Wharf were extensive quays and warehouses where the Cromford and High Peak Railway once connected with the canal; then came Lea Wood engine house, containing a beam engine to pump water into the canal from the River Derwent, and a substantial aqueduct over the river. Beyond it the canal, which had previously run through fields in a valley about half a mile wide, ran on a shelf on the hillside through woods. A small aqueduct carried it over a railway emerging from a tunnel—this line, formerly part of a main line from Manchester to London, had become no more than a single-track branch linking Matlock with Derby; from Cromford to Ambergate it was never far from the canal.

In the woods, russet fronds of bracken were emerging from the fast-dissolving snow; in the valley, a man was mowing a lawn, carefully dodging snow patches as he did so. Shortly afterwards came a short tunnel, ignored by the Ordnance Survey one inch map, and Whatstandwell produced a remarkably good lunch in the bar of a pub near the canal. Then the walk continued to Ambergate: and there, round a corner, the canal ceased abruptly; a row of piles across the channel diverted the water into a culvert, and the course of the canal beyond had become thin air, where the ground had been excavated to build a large industrial complex.

Railway stations at Cromford, Whatstandwell and Ambergate provided a convenient means for towpath walkers to return to their starting point, though possibly not many were using it ('Two and a dog from Ambergate to Cromford' said the conductor-guard. 'Don't often get asked for a fare like that'.)

The Cromford Canal was opened in 1794; its main line ran from Cromford in a south-easterly direction down the valley of the Derwent as far as Ambergate; it then went off across country to the east, passed through a one and three-quarter-mile long tunnel at Butterley and gained the upper part of the valley of the River Erewash, down which it turned to the south to reach Langley Mill where it joined the Erewash Canal (and also, a few years after opening, the Nottingham Canal; of this, though, more in the next section of this chapter). From Cromford to Ambergate is five and a quarter miles; the whole canal was fourteen and a half miles long. From Langley Mill up to Butterley the locks were built for wide boats; the tunnel and lock-free upper section fitted narrow boats only. In 1852 the canal was purchased by a railway company.

The later history of the upper section of the canal was bound up with that of Butterley Tunnel. In 1889 it suffered a bad subsidence which blocked it; it was repaired and reopened in 1893, but in 1900 a worse subsidence occurred, probably as a result of coal mining beneath it. Despite controversy, it was never reopened again. This isolated the upper part of the canal although local traffic continued to use it for some years. It was eventually legally abandoned in 1944, but much of it remained in water.

In 1961 Derbyshire County Council suggested to the Inland Waterways Redevelopment Advisory Committee that the Cromford end of the canal should be reclaimed as an amenity waterway. The committee in its recommendations in 1961 pointed out that the top six miles were attractive and had industrial and agricultural water sales, and suggested the length should be retained for boating and water supply. This recommendation was endorsed in 1965 by the BWB in *The Facts About The Waterways*.

However, nothing seemed to happen, except that Bullbridge Aqueduct, Ambergate, was destroyed in 1968 so that the road beneath it might be widened. This suggested to local people (who were eventually to form the Cromford Canal Society in March

1971) that the canal was in danger, and they approached Derbyshire County Council with a view to its acquiring and preserving
the canal. The county council had already an enlightened plan for
acquiring amenities, turning the routes of closed railways, for
instance, into footpaths and bridleways, and was ready to help.

In 1970 the county council, after a report by its countryside sub-
committee had stressed the canal's amenity potential, approached
the British Waterways Board, owner of the canal. It was suggested
that BWB should improve the canal and that the council would
then, by agreement under provisions of the 1968 Transport Act,
take the canal over and undertake its future maintenance. The
IWAAC supported these proposals.

Agreement was eventually reached between county council and
waterways board in 1973—as I write, in October, conveyancing of
the transfer is in progress—but on different lines. Transfer of the
canal was to be accompanied by a capital payment to finance its
restoration, and on completion of the transfer, management of the
canal was to be given to the Cromford Canal Society which would
restore it, with its own resources and other help, in accordance with
a policy plan settled by the county council in consultation with the
society. In general terms the policy plan provided for the canal to
be made fit for use by light man-powered craft and, from Cromford
to High Peak Wharf, for a horse-drawn boat to carry passengers.
This would involve dredging and weed clearance as far as High
Peak Wharf; from there to Ambergate, much of the weed growth
would probably be left in the interests of natural history. The towpath, already a public right of way, was to be cleared and made fit
for walkers, though having walked it from end to end I do not
recollect any particular difficulty. The county council was to provide a landscaped car park at the Cromford end of the canal, and
expected to offer a canalside building to the society for its use.

Much earlier in the proceedings members of the society had been
enabled to enter the pump house at Lea Wood near High Peak
Wharf and set to work to restore the 1849 beam engine in order to
make it workable again.

In 1973 the canal society had about fifty members, but it planned
to start a publicity campaign for members and assistance once final
agreement had been reached about restoration of the canal. Looking still further ahead, the county council envisaged that once the
restoration scheme for the canal was complete, the society would

continue to manage the canal as a countryside amenity, though detailed terms of management remained to be settled.

Great Northern Basin, Langley Mill

The canal geography of Langley Mill, on the border of Nottinghamshire and Derbyshire, is as complex as its history. First on the scene was the Erewash Canal, opened in 1779 up the valley of the River Erewash from the River Trent eleven and three-quarter miles to the south. It was not expensive to build, and, with many coal-mines in its vicinity, it became prosperous. This prompted construction of further canals. The Cromford Canal complemented the Erewash, diverging from it at the approach to its terminal basin and continuing its line northwards. The Nottingham Canal, on the other hand, was a competitor to the Erewash—it provided a more direct route between Nottingham and the Erewash Valley and, having reached it, did not join the Erewash Canal but ran northwards along the opposite side of the valley as far as Langley Mill, where it connected with the Cromford Canal just above its junction with the Erewash. The widenings of the Nottingham and Cromford Canals at this junction comprise what is now known as Great Northern Basin. (The name probably derives from that of the Great Northern Railway, former owner of the Nottingham Canal.)

All three canals at Langley Mill now belong to the British Waterways Board, but both the Cromford and Nottingham Canals have been closed and are, in the neighbourhood of Langley Mill, except for the basin and its connection to the Erewash Canal, filled in. The Erewash Canal has fared better though with, in recent years, a narrow escape from going the same way. Commercial traffic revived during the Second World War, but ceased in 1952, and when in 1954 two IWA officials navigated the Erewash Canal prior to submitting a report to the BTC Board of Survey, they reckoned that theirs was the first boat to reach Langley Mill for two years. They also passed, 'with greatest difficulty', through Langley Mill Lock on to the Cromford Canal. In 1962 the upper five miles of the Erewash Canal, from Ilkeston to Langley Mill, were abandoned by Act of Parliament; but they continued to be maintained to supply water to the lower section, and pleasure-craft, which had appeared on the canal despite its industrial countryside, continued to be allowed to use it.

In 1968, following the Transport Act of that year, the whole of the Erewash Canal except for the first mile up from the Trent became a remainder waterway. To prevent its becoming derelict, like many other canals in the region, the Erewash Canal Preservation and Development Association was formed. Its members included canal enthusiasts, anglers, local residents and local councillors, and it was administered by a committee which included representatives of these groups; by 1973 there were about 500 members and the association had as headquarters the only remaining lock cottage on the canal, which it had restored for the purpose. Some voluntary work was done on the canal and, largely as a result of the association's campaigning, in 1970 the county councils of Derbyshire and Nottingham agreed to finance restoration of the canal to cruising standard by BWB, the cost being estimated at £58,000.

Omitted from this scheme were two short sections of canal. The first of these was the terminal basin at Langley Mill. This has been leased by BWB and, filled in, has become a factory car park. This meant that at the head of the canal there were neither moorings nor a winding hole—nowhere, that is, for boats longer than the width of the canal to turn round. Also omitted from the restoration of the Erewash Canal was Great Northern Basin—the derelict junction of the Cromford and Nottingham Canals and its approach from the Erewash, under a bridge and through a derelict wide lock, the bottom lock of the Cromford Canal. It seemed to the ECPDA that the basin, if restored, would make a natural terminus to the Erewash Canal.

There were two immediate snags. The first was that Nottinghamshire County Council was proposing water channelling of the top quarter-mile of the Erewash Canal in connection with a new by-pass road, with construction of a new terminal basin at what would have become the head of the navigable canal. This proposal was eventually withdrawn. The other snag was that BWB estimated the cost of restoring basin and lock to be £24,000; this included provision of a sanitary station and an electric pump to pump water lost by use of the lock back from the Erewash Canal into the basin. The principal supply of water to the Erewash Canal enters its top pound from the River Erewash; but the basin does have another supply, from Moorgreen reservoir and originally intended for the Nottingham Canal. This contained colliery silt which settled out in the canal and made it shallow, but the problem has been alleviated since the colliery installed settlement ponds.

The reaction of the ECPDA to the BWB estimate was to restore Great Northern Basin itself.

Work started in earnest in April 1972, principally by volunteers. The lock chamber contained, in addition to the usual mud and rubbish, all four lock gates and the masonry of the toll house which once stood beside it and had been demolished. A Hy-mac excavator did good work in the lock chamber; the basin itself was dredged by JCBs, and a Smalley excavator of the WRG completed clearance of the lock and its approach. Some 4,000 tons of spoil were removed. At the lock, the old bottom gates were repaired and re-used; for balance beams, roof timbers from a demolished factory were obtained for £15 the two. The old top gates were beyond repair and second-hand gates were obtained from a derelict lock on the Nottingham Canal—Nottingham Corporation gave permission for their removal free of charge. The edges of much of the basin had to be built up with concrete blocks; and a swing bridge, which crossed what was formerly a stop lock between the Nottingham and Cromford Canals, had to be restored. When it was jacked up (using two ten-ton jacks) it was found that the balls in the ball race, on which it swung, were 4 mm. thick with rust—but still spherical. When I saw the bridge in April 1973 it was again operable, having recently been swung open for the first time in, it was thought, thirty-seven years. The basin was by then completely cleared and part-full of water; it was difficult to credit its previous state of dereliction shown by photographs. It was formally reopened on 26 May 1973.

The cost of restoration was about £2,000. When it started on its task, the association had about £50 available. It made a public appeal for £1,800; most of the money came from local authorities, but there were substantial contributions from private individuals and from the association's fund-raising activities, such as sponsored walks. A local contractor provided, free, lorries to remove dredged spoil: a contribution worth many hundreds of pounds. Heanor UDC made grants of £600 for excavation and £200 for landscaping and planting trees.

It was anticipated that BWB would lease the basin area, including the lock, to the ECPDA at a low rent; the association appointed three trustees (volunteers) to take the lease on, on its behalf.

From the date of reopening until 14 September 1973, 107 boats entered the basin, and five took up long-term moorings. The Narrow Boat Owner's Club was planning to hold its annual rally at the basin at Easter 1974. Water supply had been adequate, though there were occasions when the water level in the basin recovered, after the lock had been used, more slowly than desirable. The day-to-day supply was only from a brook which ran into the feeder, as the outlet valve of Moorgreen reservoir was normally kept closed, although the association could draw on it, with BWB's consent, for short-term supplies. The ECPDA was considering installing a pump to return water from below the lock, if only for occasional topping-up.

The ECPDA could not charge boats entering the basin before it had formally entered into the lease; it did receive some voluntary donations. It planned to charge for long-term mooring once the lease was in operation; there was to be no charge for boats to enter the basin, wind and moor temporarily—though voluntary donations would continue to be welcome!

6 · The Welsh Border

The Brecon and Abergavenny Canal

The thirty-two and a half mile stretch of the Brecon and Abergavenny Canal from Jockey Bridge, Pontypool, to Brecon has two remarkable features. Firstly, it runs through most attractive mountain scenery; secondly, it was the first canal to be restored as a result of joint action by local authorities and BWB. The first of these features contains the key to the second: this length of canal lies within the Brecon Beacons National Park, and it was National Parks legislation that enabled the county councils of Monmouthshire and Breconshire to assist British Waterways Board with finance for restoration. Immediately prior to the restoration scheme, much of the canal was already navigable by small pleasure cruisers: but the northernmost six and three quarter miles from Talybont to Brecon were rendered un-navigable by low bridges fixed across the canal.

This canal is the last navigable survivor of several which once served the South Wales valleys. Fed by many horse-drawn tramways they linked coal mines and iron works with ports; they were never connected directly with the main English canal system. The Brecon and Abergavenny retains this characteristic, being an isolated length of canal, and its locks were intended for boats of distinctive dimensions—about 60 ft. long by about 8 ft. 6 in. beam.

The canal originated in the 1790s when a canal was planned to link Abergavenny with the River Usk, which flows to the sea at Newport. At that time the Monmouthshire Canal was being built from Newport north to Pontypool, with a long branch to Crumlin; it was opened in 1796. The Monmouthshire Canal Co. persuaded the promoters of the Abergavenny canal to build their canal not to the Usk but to a junction with their own canal at Pontymoel, near Pontypool. It had also been decided to extend north-westwards from Abergavenny to Brecon—so that when the Brecknock (or

Map Eight
The Brecon and
Abergavenny Canal

Brecon
Brynich
POWYS
(Formerly Breconshire)
Pencelli
Talybont
Ashford
Crickhowell
Llangynidr
Llangattock
Abergavenny
Gilwern
Govilon
Llanfoist

GWENT
(Formerly Monmouthshire)

Goytre

Jockey Bridge

Aqueduct Lock Tunnel

Brecon and Abergavenny Canal
Monmouthshire Canal
Towns and villages
Miles
0 1 2 3 4 5

Pontypool
Pontymoel
Sebastopol

Cwmbran

Brecon) and Abergavenny Canal was eventually completed in 1812 it ran for thirty-three and a quarter miles from Pontymoel via Govilon (near Abergavenny) to Brecon, although tramways connected with it reached as far north as Hereford. From Pontymoel to Llangynidr it was laid out with one continuous pound of twenty-three miles; there are then five locks within a quarter of a mile; in the rest of the route to Brecon is only one other lock, Brynich, two miles short of the town. At Brynich also the canal crosses the Usk by a massive stone aqueduct; and at Ashford, between Brynich and Llangynidr, is a tunnel of minuscule appearance. For much of its route, the canal contours the leafy slopes of the Usk Valley, with views to the river below and high hills above.

The Monmouthshire Canal on the other hand was relatively heavily locked, with thirty-one locks in the nine miles of its main line, and passed in part through industrial surroundings. In 1865 the Brecon and Abergavenny Canal was sold to the Monmouthshire Canal Co., and in 1880 that company was amalgamated with the Great Western Railway Co. In 1948, therefore, the canal was nationalized, though for some years afterwards it came under South Wales Docks administration before passing to British Transport Waterways.

The name *Monmouthshire and Brecon Canal* had come to be used to cover both canals collectively.

By the early years of the present century commercial traffic on the Brecon and Abergavenny Canal was very light, and the last toll for it was collected in 1933. There was a little pleasure-traffic and the canal had become important for water supply, water being extracted from the Usk at Brecon and supplied to industries along the Monmouthshire Canal. In 1949 it was reported in an IWA *Bulletin* that although the B and A was not abandoned, there were no boats on it: even maintenance materials were carried by road. Toll rates were available for pleasure-craft on condition they did not use the locks. In 1952 the IWA held a rally of small craft at Brecon. In 1958, however, there were still only rowing boats and canoes on the canal; in the following year, because the channel had become so silted that water supplies were inadequate, dredging by dragline started at the lower end of the canal, a weed-cutting launch came into use, and then a few pleasure-cruisers started to appear.

13 *Upper* Passengers go aboard paddle vessel *Jane Austen* on the Kennet and Avon at Bath. August 1973. (Author)

Lower Wootton Wawen Aqueduct, Stratford Canal. May 1973. (Author)

14 *Upper* Ascending Stourbridge 16. May 1973. (Author)
Lower The diamond-shaped lock at Wyre, Lower Avon. August 1970. (Author)

During the 1950s ownership of the canal was offered to the local authorities on terms which were unacceptable to them. But members and officers of the two county councils concerned were very keen to realize the potential of the canal for recreation and amenity. The means to do so came about through the National Parks and Access to the Countryside Act. Passed as early as 1949, this act enabled local authorities to improve waterways in national parks for sailing, boating, bathing or fishing, and authorized government grants for the purpose (originally these could be up to 100 per cent, but were modified to 75 per cent by the Countryside Act 1968). From Jockey Bridge, Pontypool, to Brecon, the Brecon and Abergavenny Canal was included in the Brecon Beacons National Park, established in 1957, and the park planning committees, of the two counties, and the Brecon Beacons National Park Joint Advisory Committee opened consultations with the then National Parks Commission, British Transport Waterways and the Inland Waterways Redevelopment Advisory Committee. During 1961 the national park joint advisory committee unanimously resolved to support restoration of the canal and adopted a scheme involving financial aid (supported by government grant) from the local authorities. The scheme then went forward to the Ministry of Housing and Local Government.

Outside the national park, things were not so happy. Part of the Monmouthshire Canal had been closed for navigation in 1954, prior to construction of a new town at Cwmbran. In 1962 the rest of it was statutorily closed, and so was the Brecon and Abergavenny for about three-quarters of a mile from Pontymoel north to Jockey Bridge, although in practice both this and part of the Monmouthshire Canal have remained navigable. At the far end of the Brecon and Abergavenny, the opposite had taken place: though it continued to be a statutory navigation, it was obstructed at Talybont by a low-level bridge which had replaced a lifting bridge in about 1948. In 1964 the county planning officer of Breconshire was quoted in an IWA *Bulletin* as writing that there was no immediate prospect of the bridge being removed: the scheme prepared by local authorities awaited ministry approval, before the obstruction could be removed.

At this time, increasing numbers of motor cruisers were being placed on the canal and in 1963 a boat club was formed at Govilon. Also the then district inspector in charge of the canal was doing much to keep it open for navigation, quietly and effectively and on a shoe-string budget (although not welcoming volunteers: voluntary work has not been a feature of the National Park section of the canal).

The Facts About The Waterways had much to say about the Monmouthshire and Brecon Canal in 1965. Its future, it said, had been the subject of intense discussion involving the National Parks Commission, the Park Planning Authorities, the Welsh Office and the Ministry of Transport. The southern section, i.e. south of the national park, was maintained to water channel standards; part had been disposed of to Cwmbran UDC, the British Waterways Board retaining rights to passage of water. The northern, or national park, section was described as hardly navigable and requiring expenditure on dredging and bridges to make it navigable. Nevertheless, if maintenance were reduced to water channel standards, the annual deficit on the section could be halved: and it was anticipated that if negotiations with the Welsh Office and others proceeded satisfactorily, the board's loss would be restricted appropriately, with the other parties to the agreement providing funds to make pleasure-boating possible. Three years before the 1968 Transport Act, this line of thought seems already to foreshadow the arrangements later made for restoration of remainder waterways.

In 1967 a BWB official was quoted in the *Daily Telegraph* as describing the Brecon and Abergavenny Canal as the outstanding case for consideration for restoration. But it was not until the following year, 1968, that an agreement was concluded between the British Waterways Board and the county councils of Monmouthshire and Breconshire. The canal was to be restored from Jockey Bridge to Brecon by BWB at the cost of the county councils, which would be aided by government grant. Subsequent maintenance costs have been shared between the board, on the one hand, and the county councils jointly, on the other. Only direct costs are involved and the county councils have been meeting half of these, after being credited with the whole of the canal's income, subject in some years to minor adjustments. The county councils have met their costs, both for restoration and their share of maintenance, in the proportions Breconshire, five-eighths, Monmouthshire, three-eighths—these approximating to the lengths of the canal in each county. The BWB's annual report for 1968 pointed out that the canal was a remainder waterway but expressed the hope that once restoration was complete it would take its place among the cruising waterways—a hope which has yet, as I write, to be realized.

Restoration work commenced in 1968 when the chairman of BWB lowered a new gate into position at Brynich Lock. All gates at the lock were renewed. A floating dredger was introduced to produce adequate depth for cruising throughout the canal—particularly over lengths totalling about eleven miles which were inaccessible to the dragline. During 1970, 34,000 tons of dredgings were removed from the canal. A new steel and aluminium drawbridge was built and installed at Talybont (its design had later to be modified to make it easier to use) and four new wooden drawbridges were installed between Talybont and Pencelli—occupation bridges for farmers, former drawbridges on their sites having ceased to function.

On 16 October 1970 the canal within the national park was formally reopened by the Secretary of State for Wales. The restoration scheme had cost about £28,000; and it received a Countryside Award presented by the Prince of Wales.

South of the national park boundary the canal has become, in official terms, a water channel, maintained for water supply; it continues on the same level, however, for about three miles before the first, unusable, lock is reached. The first three-quarters of a mile to Pontymoel is used by cruisers and by maintenance craft of BWB. About three-quarters of a mile further on, on the Monmouthshire Canal, is Crown Bridge, Sebastopol, where the canal runs through a corrugated iron pipe inserted under the bridge by Pontypool UDC in 1968 in connection with road improvements. The pipe is large as pipes go but still too small for any but the smallest boats. The final mile of level canal to the lock now belongs to Cwmbran UDC. The South Wales section of the IWA has held working parties on this part of the canal to tidy it up and clean silt out and rubbish, and in doing so to attempt to impress authorities with its amenity potential; and in 1970 the IWAAC recommended restoration and promotion to cruising waterway for the Jockey Bridge to Cwmbran section—but all without result at the time of writing.

In any event, restoration and improvement of the national park section has tended to be a continuing process, since the formal reopening. More dredging has been done, for instance, and gates have been renewed in the locks at Llangynidr. Use of the canal by boats has also increased greatly. Figures for receipts and maintenance in 1972 make an interesting comparison with those for 1964 (when some boats were using the canal, but formal restoration had not started):

	1964 £	1972 £
Receipts:		
Craft	612	4,876
Water sales	61	52
Other (fishing, rents etc.)	834	1,814
	1,507	6,742
Expenditure (direct and indirect)	19,818	68,044

The county councils made a contribution towards maintenance, in 1972, of £19,866; they themselves received grants from the Countryside Commission (which has succeeded the National Parks Commission). Water sales figures do not take into account sales from the Monmouthshire Canal, although these are dependent on maintenance of the national park section.

Expenditure on the canal within the national park averaged £2,095 a mile in 1972; principal items were:

Direct costs (total £52,998): Banks and hedges, £21,363; dredging, £9,879; locks and lock gates, £3,562; bridges and aqueducts, £2,852; transport, £2,069; area section office expenses, £5,507; special maintenance, £4,764. (The last item referred to piling of banks—an inevitable consequence of introduction of powered boats where previously there were none.)

Indirect costs: Departmental administration, £9,563; headquarters administration, £3,150; rates, £1,330.

In 1973 there were three firms offering hire cruisers on the canal, and another running a waterbus on charter excursions. To visit this canal by boat rather than car remained for me an unfulfilled ambition, but that many others do cruise on it is confirmed by the rapidly increasing numbers of boats on the canal. In 1972 it averaged eight boats to a mile (compared with an average of nine a mile over the whole BWB canal system); and the figures for pleasure-boats shown in the annual BWB pleasure-boat counts are worth quoting in full: 1967, 106; 1968 (restoration scheme agreed),

107; 1969, 136; 1970 (restoration scheme completed), 203; 1971, 217; 1972, 278.

The Montgomery Canal with Something About the Llangollen Canal and the Prees Branch

When I was considering, early in 1973, which waterways could be said to be restored, and should therefore be described in this book, it seemed to me that the three-quarters of a mile of the closed Montgomery Canal through Welshpool, which was cleared out by volunteers in 1969 to the extent that a passenger-trip boat could operate, should certainly be included. Further considera-tion suggested that this short length could not be dealt with adequately in isolation, without adding a description of the whole thirty-five-mile Montgomery Canal (although this was neither restored nor, at that time, the subject of an official restoration pro-ject); and that in turn implied mention of the Llangollen Canal and its Prees Branch.

Shortly before the manuscript was due at the publisher, however, came the welcome news of firm proposals to restore a seven-mile section of the Montgomery Canal, from Welshpool northwards, and funds were being raised to restore the rest of the canal also: but a big problem, that of many lowered main road bridges, remained to be solved.

Neither of the names *Llangollen Canal* and *Montgomery Canal* appears to have much historical justification. They are now often applied (in, for instance, the BWB-published *Nicholson's Guide to the Waterways*) to those two branches of the Shropshire Union Canal of which the first leaves its main line at Hurleston Junction to run south-west to Ellesmere and Frankton Junction and then north-west to Llangollen and Llantysilio, while the second runs from Frankton Junction south-west via Welshpool to Newtown. This layout, simple on the map, has complex origins. In the 1790s the original intention—distilled from several proposals—of the promoters of the Ellesmere Canal was to build a canal from the Mersey, at the point which later became called Ellesmere Port, via Chester and industrial Ruabon to the Severn at Shrewsbury, with several branches, particularly eastwards to Ellesmere, Whitchurch and a junction with the Chester Canal (which ran from Chester to

133

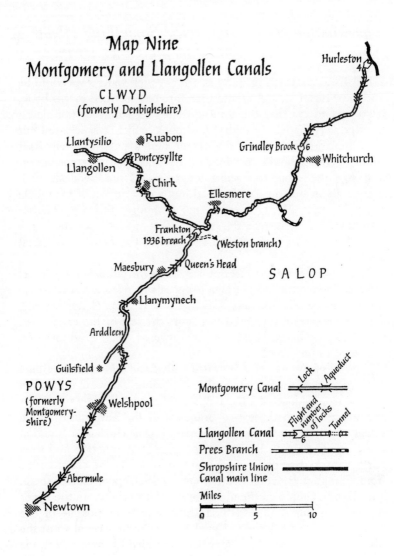

Map Nine
Montgomery and Llangollen Canals

C L W Y D
(formerly Denbighshire)

Hurleston 4

Ruabon

Llantysilio
Pontcysyllte
Llangollen
Chirk

Grindley Brook 6
Whitchurch

Ellesmere

Frankton
1936 breach
(Weston branch)

Maesbury
Queen's Head

S A L O P

Llanymynech

Arddleen

Guilsfield

P O W Y S
(formerly Montgomery-shire)

Welshpool

Abermule

Newtown

Montgomery Canal ←Lock ←Aqueduct

Llangollen Canal —Flight and number of locks 6 —Tunnel

Prees Branch

Shropshire Union Canal main line

Miles

0   5   10

Nantwich) and westwards to Llanymynech. A separate proposal, the Montgomeryshire Canal, was to extend the Llanymynech branch to Newtown.

The main line was never completed. The section from Ellesmere Port to Chester, where it joined the Chester Canal, was built; and so was the section from the north end of Telford's magnificent Pontcysyllte aqueduct, near Ruabon, southwards to Weston Wharf, nine miles short of Shrewsbury as the crow flies and probably much further by the intended canal, which was never built. A branch from Pontcysyllte to Llantysilio was built as a navigable feeder, taking water from the River Dee; the branch to Llanymynech was built, leaving the main line at the bottom of Frankton locks, and extended eventually to Newtown, with a further short branch to Guilsfield; and the branch from Frankton Junction, at the top of Frankton locks, to Whitchurch was also built, with a sub-branch which, heading for Prees, petered out after three and a half miles. When this compact little system was eventually linked to the Chester Canal, it was by the softer option of extending the Whitchurch branch to Hurleston rather than extending the main line northwards through the rugged country of the Welsh border. The whole network remained isolated from the main canal system until links were built in the 1830s. By a series of amalgamations all these canals eventually became part of the Shropshire Union Railways and Canal Company, which intended to convert many of its canals into railways but did not: it did build one quite separate branch railway and then got swept up into the giant London and North Western Railway Co. Under lease: it was not formally absorbed by that company until 1922, a few days before the LNWR itself was amalgamated into the London Midland and Scottish Railway Co.

In the meantime closure of the Llanymynech to Newtown section had been considered as early as 1887: it was making a very small profit and survived. Most of the line from Frankton to Weston became disused after a breach in the bank in 1917.

A more serious breach occurred in 1936, on the Montgomery Canal not far south of Frankton. It was not repaired: the last remaining trader on the canal received some compensation and carried on for a couple of years with local traffic beyond the breach. Breach or no, commercial traffic over the whole of the Montgomery and Llangollen Canals had ceased by the end of the thirties. In 1944, Parliament authorized their abandonment.

The Llangollen Canal, however, had to be maintained as a feeder to supply water to the Shropshire Union main line at Hurleston. The scenery of its upper reaches is attractive and its aqueducts spectacular, and after the Second World War pleasure-craft began to venture on to the canal.* (Horse-drawn tripping boats had for many years been a feature of the canal at Llangollen.) In 1947 an IWA *Bulletin* reported that L. T. C. Rolt had recently made an 'exceedingly difficult and adventurous passage as far as Ellesmere'. Others followed and despite low water levels and excessive weed succeeded in reaching Llantysilio. But in 1949 came a further threat to the canal's navigability. The act of abandonment had enabled local authorities to take over road bridges, lowering them if they wished. That year came proposals to lower three of them, including a main road bridge at Grindley Brook and another where the Ruabon–Llangollen road crossed the canal. After representations by the IWA, Llangollen town council unanimously passed a resolution, forwarded to the county councils concerned, that all bridges on the section should be kept at navigation height. Even the DIWE opposed lowering of bridges (to the surprise of the IWA) since it wished to be able to continue to move its maintenance boats along the canal. But it was not until 1952 that Denbighshire County Council decided to improve road approaches rather than lower bridges. The same year twenty-five boats attended a rally at Llangollen. By 1970 it was estimated that boats were reaching Llangollen, in summer, at a rate of 250 a week.

It was not pleasure-boat traffic that saved the canal, though. Proposals to use it as a water supply channel had been heard of as far back as 1950. It was even feared that such use might lead to restriction or prohibition of navigation. Eventually the BTC entered into an agreement with the Mid and South East Cheshire Water Board to carry water from the Dee to a reservoir at Hurleston; after the necessary works had been done, the scheme was officially inaugurated in 1959. In 1964, according to *The Facts About The Waterways*, water sale revenue on the Llangollen Canal was £43,032, and the canal produced a surplus of £6,399. There was also much use by pleasure-craft. The 1968 Transport Act scheduled this abandoned canal as a cruising waterway, and the 1972 pleasure-boat count reported more boats on the move on the

* Powers to permit pleasure-craft had been retained.

Llangollen than on any other canal. (Curiously, it linked the figures for the Llangollen and Montgomery Canals together—but, as I shall explain shortly, it seems unlikely that there were many boats moving on the Montgomery.)

Cruising on the Llangollen Canal in 1958 I did not, so far as I can recollect, notice that it was either more or less busy, or in better or worse condition, than other canals. It did produce one surprise: coming to the entrance to the Prees Branch, I expected to find the branch derelict. In fact, it was being dredged, and I was able to cruise up it without difficulty for a mile or so to a clay puddle quarry; beyond that point, reeds and weed closed in across the canal and it was impassable. The puddle quarry was clearly in use, and the activity was, I suspect, due to the water supply scheme.

In the mid-sixties quarrying ceased and the branch became virtually impassable throughout. In 1971 BWB made proposals for its future: to retain the first mile or so of the branch for navigation, to retain a further half-mile, approximately, as a nature reserve without boats, and to eliminate the rest. Work has been proceeding along these lines; and planning permission has been granted to redevelop the old clay pits as a marina with moorings for several hundred boats.

All these boats will have to have somewhere to cruise and there have already been reports of congestion on the Llangollen Canal. The obvious place to relieve this congestion would be on the Montgomery Canal. Up the valley of the Severn, among the foothills of the Welsh mountains, it is scenically almost as attractive as the Llangollen: but, abandoned at the same time, it has not fared so well since. True, in 1973 much of it remained in water, to meet obligations to provide drinking water for farm animals, and to provide land drainage (when a canal was built which interfered with natural drainage, its proprietors had by statute to provide alternative drainage). But there were also several lengths dry, or piped, or thickly grown with weed. A short terminal length at Newtown had been sold. The twenty-six narrow locks were in the condition to be expected after thirty-five years of disuse. There were lifting bridges which could no longer be lifted, and many of the other bridges had been lowered or culverted. Responsibility for maintenance of bridges had become a complex situation: accommodation bridges remained the responsibility of BWB, but maintenance of public road bridges was split between five authorities. Twelve road bridges and a railway bridge had been culverted. In six places water pipes crossed the canal with but 1 ft. 6 in. headroom—although the agreements for these pipe crossings provided that they should be either raised or put below the canal bed if navigation were restored.

I must admit that, while knowing the district through which the canal passed, I had kept something of a closed mind about the canal itself. It would clearly have been most attractive to cruise along, and it was equally clear to me that it was so hopelessly lost as to be painful to consider. Fortunately others were less pessimistic. In 1967 members of the Shropshire Union Canal Society started to think about restoration, and in June 1969 the society produced a comprehensive survey and report which advocated it.

The society, a registered charity, had been formed in November 1969 to 'promote interest in the past, present and future' of the Shropshire Union Canal. To form it, the Shrewsbury and Newport Canal Association had been reconstituted after an unsuccessful two-year campaign for restoration of that closed branch of the Shropshire Union. The Society's Montgomery campaign has been proceeding better. In 1972 the society was reformed as a company limited by guarantee; by 1973 it had about 600 members.

Soon after the society's restoration report was produced, proposals which had been formulated some years earlier were published for a by-pass road at Welshpool which was to use the route of the canal through the town. *Through* the town, not *round* it: the canal passes through the town and the by-pass was to do likewise, separating one part of it from another. To oppose it the Welshpool By-pass Action Committee was formed, and at this committee's request the SUCS and the IWA (through the *Navvies Notebook* organization) arranged, with BWB approval, a large voluntary weekend working party on the canal at Welshpool in October 1969. The immediate object of the working party was to clear out and renovate the canal through the town: this was achieved by 180 volunteers with mechanized assistance. The longer-term object was to demonstrate that the canal, instead of being a nuisance, should be retained as a valuable amenity.

As a result of this big working party—which proved to be the first of many smaller ones—the Montgomery Branch of the Shropshire Union Canal Society was formed, based on Welshpool. In 1970 the branch purchased a narrow boat converted for passenger-tripping, named it *Powis Princess*, and took it by road to Welshpool where two cranes lowered it on to the canal. Operated by members, by 1973 it had carried 11,000 passengers.

Because of opposition, a public inquiry was held in July 1971 into the by-pass proposals; and at last, in August 1972, it was made known that the Secretary of State for Wales accepted recommendations of the inspector who held the inquiry: the canal route was not to be used for the road, and other solutions were to be sought to Welshpool's traffic problems. A good decision, and one which helps to restore my sometimes faltering faith in democratic procedures.

In the meantime, much else had been going on. The IWAAC had inspected the canal and recommended that no further action be taken to jeopardize future restoration. In 1970 Montgomeryshire's county planning officer proposed partial restoration of the canal in that county—restoration of several lengths, that is, for small craft. In 1972, when it was proposed to culvert a road bridge at Abermule, protests by the SUCS and IWA were successful in altering the proposed culvert into a bridge with 6ft. 6 in. headroom for boats.

In Welshpool, the borough council obtained a grant of £10,000 from the Department of the Environment for improving the canal within the borough boundary, and this, with £2,000 provided by the council itself, made £12,000 available for clearing six miles of towpath and hedges and dredging the canal. SUCS working parties continued, and in May 1973 I found members hard at work, after advice from BWB staff, restoring Welshpool Lock. This was to enable *Powis Princess* to extend her cruising range.

SUCS volunteers had also started agricultural clearance work at Frankton locks. The society's policy was to promote full restoration of the canal (except the Guilsfield branch, now a nature reserve) by stages: the first stage being the six miles and seven locks from Frankton to Maesbury. It had produced a detailed thirteen-page survey of the work needed. This section, if reopened, would see immediate use by boats off the Llangollen; it also presented the greatest problems of restoration. Almost two miles of the canal bed was dry, past the site of the 1936 breach, where forty yards of bank were swept away and not replaced. At Queen's Head, not far south of the dry section, the canal passed beneath the A5 road in a culverted bridge. This circumstance contained the source of its own cure: there was a proposal to make the road into a dual carriageway, and the society was making representations to the road authorities (Salop County Council and the Department of the Environment) for a bridge with navigation clearance to be built as part of the road scheme. These representations were being met sympathetically—provided the society could meet a cost estimated at £16,000.

Even BWB officials cautiously expressed their opinions to me, in the spring of 1973, that in the long-term the canal would eventually be restored, and BWB had, as an exercise, made a study of the Frankton to Llanymynech section to see what would be needed if it were.

In October the same year H.R.H. the Prince of Wales, as chairman of the Prince of Wales Committee, announced that it was to give its full support to plans to restore to full amenity standards the seven-mile stretch from Welshpool to Arddleen. One of the main aims of this committee, established in 1971, was to give encouragement to groups of volunteers with practical projects for improving their environment in Wales. By giving advice, material aid and sometimes money, it had assisted schemes throughout the principality—work camps for young people, footpaths and nature trails, restoration of old buildings, work by schools and other volunteers. The canal project was much larger than any in which the committee had previously been involved.

Members of the Variety Club of Great Britain undertook to help to raise funds, with the particular aim of enabling the canal to be used by boats carrying handicapped children. Medical advice was that this slow-moving form of travel is an excellent form of therapy for many handicapped or deprived children: it enables them, as does no other method of transport, to come to very close quarters with deep countryside. An overnight hostel was also envisaged.

No big engineering problems were foreseen on the seven-mile stretch, but work was needed on dredging, bank protection, locks, removal of vegetation, and also on repairs to the feeder from the River Tanat. Cost of restoration was estimated by BWB at £250,000, after making allowance for work to be done by voluntary labour. It was intended to form a charitable trust (on which the Shropshire Union Canal Society would be represented) to provide funds for the project; this was to work in close co-operation with BWB.

For the rest of the canal, the SUCS, having obtained the services of a professional fund-raiser, then launched a separate appeal, principally to industry, for £300,000 to further its restoration. It was anticipated that voluntary labour would be used in part, particularly on the locks, the society then being about to complete restoration of Welshpool lock for £1,500, against a commercial estimate of £12,000. The appeal figure did not take into account works necessary for restoration of lowered road bridges, which remained to be negotiated; but the society's ultimate aim was restoration of the whole canal from Frankton to Newtown.

7 · Yorkshire Waterways

Linton Lock

The administration of Linton Lock is one of those curious anachronisms which enliven the study of inland waterways. In 1973 it was still owned and operated by the Linton Lock Navigation Commissioners, as it had been since it was built in 1774, though it owes its recent survival to the Linton Lock Supporters' Club.

The location, on the Yorkshire River Ouse, of this little independent navigation authority was at first sight something of a curiosity, too. It is responsible also for navigation over seven and three-quarter miles of river upstream of the lock and two miles downstream. Before the upstream boundary is reached, the river has changed its name to Ure and there becomes the River Ure Navigation, which connects in turn with the Ripon Canal. Both of these are BWB waterways and the Ripon Canal, though short (one and a quarter miles) supports a great many boats (seventy-seven were present at the 1972 pleasure-boat count, with another seventy-five on the Ure Navigation). For these, Linton Lock provides the only outlet to the rest of the inland waterways: downstream through York (where the navigation authority is the Ouse and Foss Navigation Trustees), through Naburn Locks to the tideway.

In the eighteenth century, before locks were built on the River Ouse, boats could usually ascend it as far as Linton, and sometimes further; the weir and lock there were built to enable them to continue upstream at any time. Further locks upstream were a separate undertaking, and the locks at Naburn, downstream, were a later development, leaving the Linton Lock Navigation in the middle.

The Linton Lock commissioners were set up by an Act of Parliament in 1766 which envisaged making navigable both their section of the river and several tributaries: so far as I am aware, Linton Lock is the only part of the work actually carried out. The act is a fascinating document and is, apart from a tendency to print *s* as *f*, remarkably ea*f*y to under*f*tand. The list of names of the original commissioners runs to three pages; nowadays there are only a few commissioners. When one dies or refuses to act, it is lawful for the remaining commissioners to appoint another in his place—as is done from time to time. Two provisions of the act are particularly relevant to present-day conditions: firstly, there is a right of navigation over the commissioners' river for 'all people whatsoever'; and secondly, tolls may be imposed on goods conveyed (e.g. coal at 4d a ton) but specifically not on 'Boats out upon Plea*f*ure only.'

So the disappearance of commercial craft from this part of the Ouse has left the commissioners without any income from tolls. They did operate at a profit until about 1920: then trade fell away and there were insufficient funds to maintain the lock. By 1948 the lock was no longer usable, and the Linton Lock Supporters' Club was formed by one of the commissioners to raise funds for its repair and to help provide for maintenance. About £900 was subscribed and the lock repaired. In 1960 one of the bottom gates of the lock collapsed: it was repaired by contract but it took commissioners and supporters' club some ten years to pay off the bill.

By 1962 the top gates were so bad that there was a danger of their collapsing. Cost of repairs was estimated at £6,000 to put the lock in order, and a further £4,000 to carry out essential works. These sums were far beyond the commissioners' resources: they decided to close the lock in the interest of public safety and, though unable to resign (being appointed for life), they announced that they refused to act further.

Fortunately, others were prepared to act—a most public-spirited gesture—and new commissioners were sworn in, including the then chairman of the IWA's North-eastern Branch. The supporters' club then set about raising finance for repairs to the lock, the main donors being Ripon and York Motor Boat Clubs. New top gates were made and fitted by British Waterways Board, on a non-profit basis, in May 1966, and the lock was then navigable again after an interval of four years. Even then it had to be closed from September 1966 to July 1967, because of a bad leak past the bottom gates, cured by BWB.

A visit in 1973 showed Linton Lock to be short, wide and deep: its actual dimensions are 58 ft. long and 15 ft. wide—typical of waterways of the North of England—with a fall which varies according to river levels but is about 8 ft. 6 in. As elsewhere there was nothing in particular to show its unusual circumstances. Beside the lock was a lock cottage, now let, and opposite was the lock island, a weir with an impressive fall of water and a concrete building beside it which was once a small hydroelectric generating station. Below the weir, the river flow was eroding the lock island alongside the lock: an old barge had been moored to act as a breakwater, but a permanent solution was expected to cost many thousands of pounds.

The electricity generating station left a legacy of trouble to the navigation. When it was built, about 1920, water-level above weir and lock was raised by about two feet to provide a head of water for the turbines. After it became disused, following the Second World War, riparian landowners wanted the level lowered again for land drainage. This was not possible because the lock cut had silted up and the navigation commissioners could not afford to dredge it. Eventually, I learned in 1973, after persuasion by the supporters' club the Central Electricity Generating Board and the river authority have agreed to do the dredging needed, after which it was planned that water-level would be lowered.

The commissioners employed no staff apart from their clerk. In addition to work done by BWB, dredging was done by contract, and some voluntary maintenance was done by supporters' club members—painting the lock gates, for instance, and cleaning them (winter floods deposit sand on the timbers, in which weeds would grow and, eventually, damage the woodwork). The commissioners have been able to obtain revenue from sources other than tolls: from fishing rights, and from leasing part of the lock cut and island to the flourishing Linton Locks Marina. By 1973, about thirty small crafts were moored there. Even if the commissioners did have powers to licence or charge pleasure-craft, it seems probable that the cost of enforcement would absorb so much of the revenue that there would be very little benefit. They were getting no support from local authorities, though some was anticipated.

So the supporters' club, with about 300 members paying an annual subscription of 50p, (raised to £1 for 1974), remained the principal means of raising funds when needed. The suggestion was

15 *Upper* Welford Wharf, at the end of the Welford Arm of the Grand Union Canal. September 1972. (Author)
Lower Grand Western Canal at Halberton, Devon. August 1973. (Author)

16 Temporary termini. *Upper:* Lack of lower gates prevents progress through Stamford Bridge Lock, Yorkshire Derwent. May 1973 .(Author)
Lower Non-swing bridge prevents progress along the Pocklington Canal at Storwood. May 1973. (Author)

made to me that it would be advantageous if the Linton Lock Navigation were taken over by BWB: but I must admit that it seemed to me that this might be a move from frying-pan to fire. Certainly BWB staff at local level have been helpful over repairs to the lock, and if this could be put on a regular footing, well and good; but the long-term survival of the lock might well be less secure as part of the nationalized waterway system, that plaything of politicians, than it has proved to be under the commissioners, whose authority is now in its third century. And to disband so ancient and august a body as the Linton Lock Navigation Commissioners would in my opinion be comparable to dismantling some valued physical survival, an aqueduct, perhaps, or pumping station, of the same great waterway era. At any rate it was hoped to celebrate the bicentenary in 1975.

The Yorkshire Derwent

On the borders of North Yorkshire and Humberside a new inland cruising system of some forty-five miles is being created where previously there was nothing. A visit by boat and car in 1973 (at which time the whole area was still Yorkshire) suggested that in scenery and surroundings it will be attractive enough to deserve popularity with boating people.

To say that previously there was nothing is not strictly accurate. Previously there was a tidal river navigable with some difficulty and two almost unusable inland navigations leading out of it. Three separate schemes made up the whole

The first is construction of a barrage, with lock for navigation, across the River Derwent at Barmby on the Marsh, where it enters the Ouse. Both rivers here are tidal; construction of the barrage will make the lowest fifteen and a half miles of the Derwent, to Sutton Lock, non-tidal. The barrage was being built by the Yorkshire River Authority (from April 1974 the Yorkshire Water Authority) for water supply, but it would greatly improve navigation over this part of the river.

The second scheme is restoration of navigation works over twenty-two and a half miles of the Derwent upstream from Sutton Lock to Malton; and the third is restoration of most of the Pocklington Canal, which connects with the Derwent at

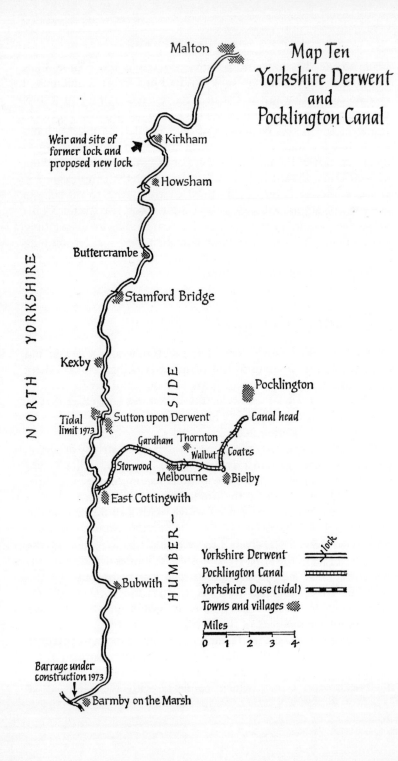

Malton

Map Ten
Yorkshire Derwent
and
Pocklington Canal

Weir and site of
former lock and
proposed new lock

Kirkham

Howsham

Buttercrambe

Stamford Bridge

NORTH YORKSHIRE

Kexby

SIDE

Pocklington

Tidal
limit 1973

Sutton upon Derwent

Canal head

Gardham   Thornton
Storwood   Walbut   Coates
Melbourne   Bielby
East Cottingwith

HUMBER

Yorkshire Derwent
Pocklington Canal
Yorkshire Ouse (tidal)
Towns and villages

lock

Bubwith

Miles
0   1   2   3   4

Barrage under
construction 1973

Barmby on the Marsh

East Cottingwith on the section still, at the time of writing, tidal.

The lower part of the Derwent passes through a flat, wide-open countryside reminiscent of the Fens; further north, it passes between rolling hills and then, at Kirkham, starts to thread a narrow winding tree-hung valley to reach Malton. The non-tidal part of the river was made navigable under an Act of Parliament of 1702, and five short and wide locks were built: Sutton (also called Elvington), Stamford Bridge, Buttercrambe, Howsham and Kirkham. The navigation came into railway ownership in 1854 and commercial traffic seems to have died out in the early years of this century—though some pleasure-traffic remained. Then in 1935 the River Derwent Navigation Act Revocation Order was made under the Land Drainage Act 1930 by the Ministry of Agriculture and Fisheries at the instigation of the River Ouse Catchment Board, which took over the navigation works in the interests of land drainage.

The catchment board had no powers to maintain navigation works, but it did not prohibit navigation either. When the top gates of Sutton and Stamford Bridge Locks became dangerous in the late thirties, they were replaced not by fixed weirs but by guillotine lock gates which, opening vertically, could not only be used as sluices to control water-levels but also allowed boats to pass. Sutton Lock continued to be used, and pleasure-craft were able to leave the tidal part of the river to seek safe moorings above the lock, until 1951; notices were then placed on moored boats by the Yorkshire Ouse River Board (the usual succession of catchment board, river board, etc., occurred here as elsewhere) saying that the (lower) gates of the lock were unsafe and that from 1 June it would be permanently closed. Before then the other four locks had also become impassable.

The IWA made an attempt to revive the navigation in the late fifties: Derwent Navigation Trustees were appointed who in 1959 entered into an agreement with the river board. But this attempt proved stillborn.

In 1969, when plans for the barrage at Barmby were announced, the North-eastern Branch of the IWA decided to have another go. It promoted a guarantee company, The Yorkshire Derwent Trust Ltd., which was incorporated on 25 September 1970, and registered as a charity. Its principal aims are preservation, improvement and management of the River Derwent as a navigation for the use of the public. After negotiations the new trust in September 1971 entered into an agreement with the Yorkshire River Authority which replaced the 1959 agreement and entitles the trust to restore the locks etc. on the river at its own expense and to use them for navigation, subject to certain protecting clauses—the river authority reserved the right to lower water-levels for land drainage, and the trust is not to interfere with the river authority's statutory powers. So far as the physical work of restoration is concerned, the trust consults with the river authority's engineers and works to their approval.

As the trust was set up as an instrument of the IWA's North-eastern Branch, all members of its council are appointed by the branch committee, and the total number of trust members allowed for is only twenty-five. To enable the public to play a part in restoration, and to promote interest in the navigation, the trust established the Yorkshire Derwent Society in 1971. By autumn 1973 it had about 150 members, mostly resident in Yorkshire. The society is managed by a committee elected by its members, to which the trust also appoints two members; and the council of the trust did include one member who represented the views of the society.

These arrangements have ensured that restoration of the Derwent, in its early stages, had the benefit of being administered by persons both experienced in waterways and financially disinterested. But from study of comparable organizations, I fear that in the long run this three-body (IWA/trust/society) set-up might have excessive scope for difficulties of communication and coordination. Elsewhere all their functions are performed successfully by a single body—on the Lower Avon for instance by the Lower Avon Navigation Trust. But the Derwent arrangements seem to have been working well in practice.

The Yorkshire Derwent Trust has estimated that restoration of the navigation would cost a sum of the order of £100,000 at commercial rates, though it anticipates that this can be much reduced by using voluntary labour. It operates a scheme for covenanted donations.

The trust got off to a good start in 1971 when an anonymous IWA member offered to pay for new lower gates for Sutton lock 'in memory of a wonderful father'. This enabled the lock to be reopened on 27 August 1972, which in turn enabled boats to reach Stamford Bridge, six and a half miles upstream. Here, too, the lock chamber remained in good condition and needed only a new pair of lower gates, and the trust had plans to build these itself. The lock was formerly a staircase, the lower chamber having been added (at an angle to the original chamber, which gives it an unusual appearance) to enable deep-laden commercial craft to pass through the lock without deepening the original chamber which is built on rock. Relatively shallow-draught pleasure-craft are not expected to need the lower chamber. Just above the lock a low bridge, formerly opening but now fixed, required restoration. Near the next lock, Buttercrambe, the river authority built a gauging weir in 1973: and although, unlike Roxton on the Great Ouse, the scheme did not produce a new lock also, it did involve clearing out the old lock chamber and cuts—the river was diverted through them while the weir was being built. Howsham lock has provided most scope so far for voluntary working parties organized by the trust. When I visited one the lock cut and chamber had been cleared of undergrowth and a farming supporter was using his forklift-equipped tractor to hoist up the coping stones from one side of the lock chamber so that roots of bushes, which had grown in the interstices of the stonework and were damaging it, could be extracted. The weir also needed repairs. Kirkham Lock presented the biggest problem: its site has been obliterated by new sluices. There was a piece of land on the opposite side of the river which it was thought would be a suitable site on which to build a new lock: and this, in its own way, is a benefit, for the river here formed the boundary between the East and North Ridings of Yorkshire, the site for the new lock was in the North Riding, a development area, and that enabled the English Tourist Board to promise £10,000 towards its cost.

Reopening of Sutton lock was followed by a rally at Stamford Bridge attended by forty-five boats. When I visited the river in May 1973, however, my lock pass was only the second to be issued for the year. I saw one other visiting boat on the move—it arrived at Stamford Bridge under sail—and a few cruisers at moorings. During 1973, up to mid-September, only twelve lock passes were issued. Other craft probably used the lock without payment, through ignorance of their owners. The principal reason why more boats did not visit the Derwent was probably that the extent of non-tidal cruising water was still very short compared with the rather unpleasant and possibly dangerous tidal approach. There was also a shortage of temporary moorings—at the time of my visit the only ones were in the lock cut at Sutton and in the lock chamber at Stamford Bridge. The trust had in fact been discouraging craft from seeking moorings on the Derwent while it collaborated with the planning authorities to bring about a scheme for providing boating facilities. It was particularly anxious to avoid the proliferation of linear moorings to be seen on other waterways.

In the long run the attractions of the Derwent deserve to become well known to boating people and will I am sure become so. They are confirmed by continued use by pleasure-craft of reaches of the river between disused locks. These were to be seen particularly between Stamford Bridge and Buttercrambe, and between Kirkham and Malton. There were in 1973, I was told, about ten small cruisers on that attractive but isolated seven-mile reach.

The Pocklington Canal

I woke, suddenly and fully, at five a.m. on a May morning to hear the whirr of snipe drumming as they flew above the boat, while swallows chittered on a branch nearby. The Pocklington Canal at East Cottingwith is bordered by Wheldrake Ings nature reserve. To check that my watch was truthful, for it was already quite light, I switched on the wireless; and then, I regret to say, switched it off again and went back to sleep, to rise drowsily at eight.

The cruising possibilities of the canal were still limited, even though its lowest lock at Cottingwith had been reopened, and when we moved off it was to pass down through the lock into the Derwent. We did later navigate the canal for the available mile or so to Storwood; but even this short journey was not simple. Floating sedge in clumps became thicker and thicker, joined forces with the widening fringe along each bank and closed across the canal. We attempted to paddle the boat, we prodded and pulled with the boathook against dense patches of sedge, my wife bow hauled and I did something nasty to the engine's cooling system. At one point our exertions took the boat bodily over the top of some sedge (it cleaned the bottom off wonderfully); and it took almost one and a half hours to reach Storwood, where we encountered the first of several too-low bridges which once had opening spans.

That section of the canal was due to be dredged, and car-borne visits showed other pounds to be in better condition. Restoration, though, was still in its early stages. It is best considered in the light of the previous history of the canal. This was opened by the Pocklington Canal Company in 1818 from Cottingwith to Canal Head, which is about a mile from Pocklington town. There are short arms to the villages of Melbourne and Bielby. In its nine and a half miles the canal has nine locks, of which five are concentrated in the last one and three-quarter miles before the terminus. In 1847 the canal was purchased by a railway company, and so descended eventually to the British Waterways Board.

The last commercial traffic was a load of roadstone in 1932: so badly was the canal silted that most of it had to be off-loaded into lighters. The last recorded pleasure-craft visited the canal in 1934. In 1959 came a proposal—fortunately unsuccessful—that the canal should be filled in with sludge to be dumped over thirty years; another proposal, in 1960, that it should be transferred to the Yorkshire Ouse River Board was equally unsuccessful; as was a proposal for restoration made in 1962 by the North-eastern Branch of the IWA and the York Angling Association. What did happen in 1962 was that the canal's eight swing bridges were replaced by fixed spans; but there remained a statutory right of navigation over the canal until this was extinguished by the 1968 Transport Act, following which it became a remainder waterway.

The restoration scheme for the canal has resulted from the activities of the Pocklington Canal Amenity Society. This society originated when farmers Eric and Doreen Lount moved into the district from the coast and found in the conspicuous absence of boats from the canal a marked contrast with what they had seen elsewhere. Following one or two small meetings in 1968 the Pocklington Canal Amenity Society was formed on 1 January 1969. To include the word *amenity* in its title was decided upon from the start, to give the society wide appeal. Apart from its potential for navigation, the canal was a good if neglected coarse fishery, and was rich in wild life. The main object of the society was to advocate development and promotion of the waterway to fullest uses, and the society became registered as a charity. Membership had grown to about 450 members by 1973, of whom about one-third lived locally.

In 1969 the society published a detailed and well-produced booklet: *The Pocklington Canal—The Case for Restoration.* This includes a description of the condition of the canal at that time. The water course was unobstructed, though in some pounds water-level was kept low and the whole canal needed dredging. Almost all the lock gates needed to be replaced and the masonry of some locks needed repairs. The fixed swing bridges needed to be restored—all were accommodation bridges for neighbouring land-owners (the canal is fortunate in that no main roads cross it and it has only four bridges carrying public roads). The canal passed through unspoilt countryside but was within forty miles of expanding urban areas—around Hull to the east and York and Leeds to the west. It was estimated that it could be restored for £44,000.

Late in 1969 the IWAAC inspected the canal and recommended restoration and promotion to cruising waterway status.

There then followed long and intricate negotiations between the society, the BWB, and local authorities (East Riding County Council and Pocklington RDC). While these were going on, the society started regular voluntary working parties on the canal, in close co-operation with BWB. Work included removing trees from both towpath and canal-bed, clearance of locks and repairs to brick-work. Some dredging was done by BWB staff. In 1971, with financial assistance in the form of £500 raised by the PCAS, BWB restored Cottingwith lock, which was officially reopened in July of that year. This enabled moorings off the tidal Derwent to be established at East Cottingwith and in 1973 half a dozen boats were moored there regularly. Other small craft were using isolated lengths of the canal.

Negotiations with authorities dragged on for so long that the society started to think of moves towards taking the canal over itself. But eventually firm restoration plans were made known in 1973. Not, unfortunately, plans for restoration to full navig-ability throughout: the difficulty is water supply. The Pocklington Canal has no reservoirs. It derives a supply of water from natural watercourses, becks which enter the canal at Canal Head and below Thornton lock, four miles lower down. Supplies at Canal Head (where the terminal pound is only about 200 yds. long) were probably adequate for infrequent use of the canal by commercial craft—say once or twice a week. They would be unlikely to be so for more intensive use by pleasure-craft, which could be anticipated were this section restored.

What was planned was restoration of the canal to full navigational cruising standards from its junction with the Derwent to
Coates lock, seven and three-quarter miles and four locks (though
even so, cruising may have to be restricted over the upper two and
a half miles from Thornton to Coates locks); the remaining one and
three-quarter miles to Canal Head were to be retained for water
supply and developed as a fishery—but the five locks on this
section were, regrettably, to be turned into cascades. It is to be
hoped that this will be done in such a way that eventual restoration,
should water supply difficulties be solved, is not made impossible.
In the meantime, navigation over four-fifths (or thereabouts) of
the Pocklington Canal is better than none at all.

Total cost of the scheme was estimated at just over £83,000,
shared between BWB and the county council. Financial arrangements had not been fully resolved in mid-1973, but the council
agreed to make an initial payment of £12,000 during its financial
year ending March 1974. This enabled plans to be made to complete dredging of the canal in 1973 (as I write, in October, it is well
under way), and to restore Gardham and Thornton locks in 1974.

Value of voluntary labour supplied by the PCAS prior to
announcement of the restoration scheme was estimated at £6,000.
With finance for the restoration scheme largely to be met by BWB
and local authority grants, the society was holding its funds
available for unseen contingencies. It also pledged itself to assist
restoration by re-seeding the banks. This task, which sounds
simple, in fact meant purchasing £200-worth of seed for 1974 and
was going to involve tractors, harrows, rollers etc.

It was hoped to start rebuilding the swing bridges in 1974
(though in late 1973 the matter was still the subject of discussion
between BWB and local authorities) and possibly to eliminate
some. All being well, it was thought that boats might reach
Melbourne the summer of 1975.

8 · Restoration Future

A prominent member of one of the oldest established voluntary waterway organizations remarked, when I went to visit him in course of preparing this book, that he did not see how I could describe fully the restoration of his waterway, since I had not been there at the time.

A very good point, as they say. But no one person could write the inside story of all restored waterways from personal experience.

What I have found as I travelled about, and have attempted to describe, were a series of waterway restoration undertakings at all the various stages of their development. In 1973 the Yorkshire Derwent, for instance, had reached, more or less, the stage reached by the Lower Avon in 1951 or the Upper Avon in 1969; the Montgomery Canal that of the lower Peak Forest in about 1971, and the lower Peak Forest that of the southern Stratford about 1963. Looking at all these waterways at approximately the same time gives an idea of how each has developed in the past and how each is likely to develop in the future, and also shows up the similarities and differences between them.

Though I have included all the principal restored waterways, there are others, of limited extent, which should perhaps have been described. Dilham Dike, for instance, in the Norfolk Broads region, has been restored by the efforts of the East Anglian Waterways Association. There is no shortage of schemes for further waterway restoration and some of them have made physical progress. As I write, a massive dig is taking place on the Droitwich Canal. The Basingstoke Canal has long been a bone of contention. The short branch of the Grand Union which leads to Old Stratford has its supporters.

But to describe waterways so briefly is undesirable. It is insufficiently informative to benefit the general reader, and it leads to resentment among protagonists of particular schemes which, they feel, should have been fully described. I shall stop here.

One thing did become clear from my observations and investigations. Just as by the early nineteenth century some canals had lived up to the glowing predictions of their promoters and become prosperous, and others had failed to do so, so in much the same way, by 1973, some restored waterways had become busy, popular for cruising and financially satisfactory, but others had become less so. I wish that there were more sign that promoters of restoration schemes would indulge in a bit more in the way of detailed market research before making their proposals public.

It is an intriguing exercise to consider briefly some of the features of the most promising type of waterway for restoration. To be financially satisfactory in the long run it must attract many boats to moorings, with the annual licence fees that result. The boats will be used, principally, for day-trips at weekends, which means that the pounds, or reaches on a navigable river, must be long enough and the locks infrequent enough to make a day's outing worthwhile and enjoyable. There is little point in spending the morning going down a flight of locks only to spend the afternoon coming back up again. Then the waterway should also have enough features of interest to attract holiday-makers on hired cruisers. It should be of sufficient general interest or concern to attract national support by volunteers during restoration, and of sufficient particular interest to encourage development of a corps of long-term volunteers (including boat-owners) to help maintain it after restoration.

This is not to say that a waterway which falls short of these criteria is unworthy of restoration. A disused and heavily-locked canal in an urban area is still likely to be better restored than destroyed, particularly if it provides a link from one part of the waterway network to another. Public money is going to be involved for both restoration and maintenance, and it is better that it should be employed constructively, towards ends from which people gain positive benefit, rather than solely to alleviate a nuisance.

There have been indications that, where public money for waterway restoration and maintenance is concerned, the source is increasingly going to be local rather than central government. In this and related fields, such as roads and railways, the trend is for central government to pass the costs on down the line to local government, from taxpayer to ratepayer. But neither source can be relied upon to last for ever, which makes continuing voluntary support all the more important.

Perhaps I am labouring a point. There is a justifiable argument that the cost of providing an amenity for all—such as navigable inland waterways—should be met from central public funds. It is my personal and matter-of-fact opinion that the closer maintenance of navigation works comes to being paid for by their boating users (in cash, kind or voluntary labour) the better are their chances of survival: and that this is, where possible, an objective for which to strive.

In any event, more waterways are going to be restored—for just as long as pleasure-cruising continues to increase, and for as long as the sight of an un-navigable half-dead waterway continues to move those who are reluctant to see an asset wasted. Which seems like quite a long time.

Appendix 1
Recent Developments

Restoration of waterways is a fast-developing subject, and inevitably there have been developments of importance during the interval between completing the text of this book and passing the proofs. These are described below.

Inland Waterways Association
In 1974 the National Waterways Restoration Fund reached its target of £50,000—and continued open.

The council of the IWA decided to establish a Restoration Committee to act as a co-ordinating committee for all restoration efforts.

Upper Avon
Ten years after reopening the Stratford Canal, H.M. the Queen Mother returned to Stratford-upon-Avon to reopen the Upper Avon Navigation. The ceremony took place on 1 June 1974 at Stratford Lock.

Amalgamation of the Upper and Lower Avon Navigations was being considered.

Kennet and Avon Canal
In the eleven years to 30 November 1973, the Kennet and Avon Canal Trust had raised £110,699 towards restoration of the waterway. About £85,000 of this was net income, i.e., subscriptions, covenants, etc, less costs of administration, and £25,000 was local authority grants. A total of £86,750 had been spent on restoration, including £23,250 in the year ended 30 November 1973.

Restoration work continued in 1974, particularly between Hungerford and Crofton, and work started on the remaining un-restored section of Widcombe flight.

Great Ouse
Work on the new lock at Great Barford started in March 1974, and volunteers organized by the Great Ouse Restoration Society and the Inland Waterways Association assisted with demolition of the remains of the old lock.

Ashton and lower Peak Forest Canals
The Ashton and lower Peak Forest Canals were officially reopened on 13 May 1974 by Dennis Howell M.P., Minister of State at the Department of the Environment; they had been usable since 1 April. Total cost of restoration was £412,000, part of which was met by government grants. At the opening ceremony the chairman of British Waterways Board announced that the Minister of State would be invited to upgrade the two canals to cruising waterways, and subsequently, according to *Waterways News*, urged the government to upgrade a total of nearly eighty miles of restored remainder waterway to cruising waterway status.

Montgomery Canal
H.R.H. the Prince of Wales visited the Montgomery Canal on 23 May 1974. He met volunteers of the Shropshire Union Canal Society and the Waterway Recovery Group at work, and then, at Welshpool, declared the lock open to navigation again by raising the paddles of the top gate and, when the chamber was full, pushing the gate open.

Llangollen Canal, Prees Branch
Preliminary announcements were made in the spring of 1974 of the opening of Whixall Marina, with moorings for 300 boats.

Pocklington Canal
By mid-1974 five and three-quarter miles of canal from Cottingwith to the tail of Thornton Lock had been dredged to full depth—6 ft. 6 in. Gardham and Coates locks were being restored. Humberside County Council made a grant of £21,810 towards the canal restoration scheme for the year 1974-5, and North Wolds District Council made a grant of £100 to the Pocklington Canal Amenity Society. In each instance there were hopes of more to come, and the society also had hopes once again of eventual restoration to navigability of the entire canal.

Grantham Canal

Some progress has been made towards restoration of this canal, which has been legally abandoned since 1936 but is still mostly in water. The canal, thirty-three and a half miles long with eighteen wide locks, runs from the Trent, near Nottingham, to Grantham. Except for the first half-mile, which is owned by the Severn-Trent Water Authority, the canal is owned by British Waterways Board. The Grantham Canal Society was formed in 1970 and re-named the Grantham Canal Restoration Society in 1972; achievements include restoration of the first lock, Trent Lock, to working order, with a rally of boats held on the canal above it in 1973, and rallies of small craft on other sections of the canal. Problems include vandalized locks and lowered bridges.

Appendix 2
Managing Canals

(Extracted and abridged from 'The Facts about the Waterways', published by British Waterways Board, 1965)

We think it is important to set down an account of what is involved
in the day-to-day running of inland waterways. Indeed we feel that
such an account is necessary because there is a good deal of popular
misconception about the facts.

The basic misconception is that canals can satisfactorily be run
with relatively little effort by any person or group of people who are
minded to apply themselves to the task. Perhaps the familiar summer picture of the tranquil canal scene leads to the belief that canal
management is an equally halcyon and uncomplicated affair. The
misconception is one which can easily give rise to quite erroneous
ideas both about costs and about organizations.

Many of the problems peculiar to canal administration spring
essentially and quite simply from geography and history. Every
mile of canal represents a ribbon of property ownership—with two
miles of boundary—stretching across the countryside. At the time
of its construction, the route cut artificially both across natural
features (streams, ditches, roads and so on) and through the
property of other parties. The many and varied conditions, upon
which the canal proprietors were permitted to build their waterways and to construct works interfering with natural flows of
water, were incorporated in the enabling Acts of the canals concerned. The position of artificial canals in these respects is different
from that of natural rivers, which normally constitute no ribbon of
separate land ownership and have formed since time immemorial
a natural boundary between the lands they separate.

There are, therefore, very many ways in which the work and
interests of adjoining landowners, local authorities and public
undertakings impinge on the canals simply because of physical
coexistence. Every landowner has, of course, his own responsibilities for boundaries and coexistence, but in the case of canals the

difference is not only one of degree but also of historical and legal complexity.

Canal Maintenance

Dealing first with engineering aspects of canal administration, every length of navigation (and this *does* apply to canalized rivers as well as artificial canals)—with its locks and weirs, towing-paths, embankments, bridges and tunnels, aqueducts, culverts, reservoirs and feeder intakes—presents its daily batch of problems ranging from simple (but often immediate) tasks of engineering maintenance or water control to relationships with adjoining property owners and the general public.

Canal maintenance and operation is a job where those responsible —and this means local staff on the canal bank in the first instance —have to be ready to turn out at any hour of the day and night, winter and summer. That is why there must be a full-time organization and labour-force, resident in the vicinity and with local community contact and information. It must, moreover, be an organization which has the collective knowledge and discipline to handle matters with certainty and speed. Troubles can arise from a variety of causes of which wind and weather are not the only ones outside the Board's control. Staff on the spot with the knowledge of when and where to detect impending trouble at vulnerable points can make all the difference between minor inconvenience and—for instance—serious flooding.

The normal engineering maintenance work needs also a number of physical services or facilities in its support. Chief among these are the repair yards, which in the Board's organization are responsible for the maintenance of all plant and equipment, pumping and other machinery, craft and vehicles. They also hold at readiness reserves of plant and equipment for use on special or emergency duties (e.g. breaches, ice-breaking, diving, etc.). There are also the pile-making workshops, at which concrete piles specially designed for bank protection are manufactured very economically, and lock gate workshops specializing in the manufacture and repair of lock gates of all types. Experience has confirmed beyond doubt the advantages in efficiency and economy which lie in organizing such facilities on a co-ordinated or regional basis rather than locally.

In carrying out programmes of maintenance work the Board

have a flexible approach and either perform the work with their own staff, or alternatively, place it to contract where this is appropriate and economic. They have also had the benefit of the co-operation of some voluntary societies in working on some of the relatively neglected waterways. Such ventures in partnership may —subject to what is decided about general policy—become an increasing feature of the canal scene. If they do, it would be welcomed by us and by many people and organizations. It is, however, in no way to underestimate the useful work of this nature that is being—and could be—undertaken, to say that neither contractors nor voluntary private organizations could be expected to be available at all times to meet all the problems of day-in-day-out physical management; nor could they be expected to hold at readiness at all times the reserves of specialized equipment to deal with them.

Quite apart from the special problems which arise in an emergency, it is of interest to note that a typical fifty-mile length of canal requires a ground organization to undertake work to the value of some £30,000/£50,000 per annum and deploying the services of some twenty-five to forty men throughout the year. The Board's total maintenance expenditure is of the order of £2 million per annum.

Track Control and Operations

Over and above the many aspects of local canal maintenance which —for all their importance and potential urgency—normally pass unnoticed, there is a range of functions inherent in the existence of a navigation (either canal or river) which may best be described as 'track control and operation'.

Among these are water control in all its aspects; the manning and operation of locks (including mechanized locks on the busy routes), weirs and swing bridges; the arrangement and publication of stoppages for special maintenance and lock repairs, etc.; the physical and statutory arrangements for dealing with craft sunk, stranded or abandoned in the waterway; implementation of the canal by-laws; matters connected with bridge loadings, the routing of heavy loads, and so on, and the safety of the waterway in abnormal circumstances.

As regards water control, for example, it will be appreciated that water supplies are drawn in varying quantities from such sources as reservoirs, streams and feeders, pumped sewage effluent and mine waters, and lockage waters from higher levels of the canal itself. These sources are not of unlimited capacity and have to be regulated and husbanded—or on occasion safely disposed of—according to prevailing circumstances. Decisions on water control have therefore to be taken daily—and perhaps hourly—to provide the right amount of water for lockage, industrial and other supplies, compensation water, evaporation and seepage losses, feed to lower levels and so on.

Virtually the whole of these track control duties has this factor in common: that in addition to local action there is a need for co-ordination over a far wider area to ensure the efficiency of the waterway system as a whole and provide the optimum service to its various classes of user. Thus to take water control as an example, it is well known that many of the summit supplies can be routed in opposite directions at will. The growing national importance of the prudent use of water resources means that this flexibility—and the resultant need to make sound practical day-to-day judgments—is tending to become more important—especially perhaps in the Midlands. Similarly, lock-opening times and lock maintenance stoppages need careful pre-arrangement and publication over a wide area to ensure the minimum of inconvenience, not only to craft, but also from the point of view of the maintenance of industrial water supplies. The need for co-ordination of such matters above local level need not be laboured.

Property Management

Besides the problem of maintaining and operating the canal track, there are a whole range of matters in which canal administration impinges upon other parties, purely because the canals are there.

The point to be stressed is the volume of work—invariably of a time-consuming nature and requiring the exercise of professional skill but usually quite unremunerative—which arises from the problems of the 'ribbon of ownership' already mentioned.

There is, for instance, the negotiation of way-leaves, easements or licences to local authorities, statutory undertakings and other bodies or individuals in respect of rights to be granted over or under, across or along, the site of the canal. They include electricity and telephone cables; gas pipes, water pipes and oil pipes; drainage and effluent pipes and discharges; bridge crossings, access, gateways, windows and rights of light; boundary definitions, encroachments, rights of support; in addition there are, of course, minor permits to be granted for such facilities as cycling, walking, filming and so on.

In every case suitable arrangements need to be made to safeguard the interests of the Board and the safety of the waterway and its users, both during construction and after. A pipe crossing, for example, may involve detailed arrangements for a temporary stoppage of the navigation; interruption to traffic has to be minimized and the continuity of water supplies assured.

Some 500 or more formal agreements of these types are negotiated and completed every year, but the number of inquiries and investigations is much larger. The revenue obtained—usually in the form of a continuing annual acknowledgment which also serves to ensure that the need for the facility and the observance of its conditions are regularly reviewed—is, for a number of reasons, often only small in relation to the administrative effort expended.

There is also the important and increasing work of safeguarding the Board's interests in regard to planning and land use. The Development Plans prepared by local planning authorities under the Town and Country Planning Acts need to be examined and kept under review. The planning applications by owners of adjoining lands where development is envisaged must be examined and, if need be, criticized. Questions also arise under the National Parks and Access to the Countryside Act—often relating particularly to public rights of way over the Board's property. Proposed registrations of freehold and leasehold interests in land held by third parties are examined with the co-operation of the Land Registry. With some 2,000 miles of waterway straddling the country, involvement in matters of this nature is very considerable indeed.

With the great increase of road construction and improvement, the waterways are much involved with the Ministry of Transport, the highway authorities and consultants acting on their behalf in the study of schemes for new motorways and trunk roads, realignments, bridge widenings and similar works impinging on the canals. Discussions with the authorities or consultants concerned take place throughout the planning and design stages until detailed plans and drawings of the work are approved. When the work is put in hand it is necessary, in collaboration with the contractor, to supervise the detailed arrangements for works affecting the waterway.

Similar considerations apply to the examination of other local authority schemes (e.g. sewerage and drainage). Also, construction works on sites adjoining the waterway often have engineering implications to be agreed with the authority and contractor concerned. Again, water undertakings—many of whose supplies derive from the same original sources as those on which the waterways rely—are increasingly looking further afield for means to augment their available resources. Applications for permanent or temporary increases of supply need to be carefully and sympathetically examined in the light of the Board's own requirements and statutory rights. As a final example, special mention must be made of the Board's close and indeed intricate relationships with river authorities: in addition to water supply the waterways perform important functions with regard to land drainage, fishing and amenities with which the river authorities are intimately concerned.

Constant liaison is needed within the local communities through which the canals pass. Access to the towpath in urban areas gives rise to many problems. Many of the Board's officers are constantly engaged in the very difficult—and very important—problems connected with the safety of children, for whom water has such a strong fascination. There are the problems (often intractable) of vandalism and nuisance; the obtaining of evidence on which to base a proscution under the Canal By-laws; and so on. These and many kindred problems, arising particularly in industrial areas and especially on canals no longer in transport use, require investigation in conjunction with local authorities, civil police or others as the case may be, to ensure their solution on a 'good neighbour' basis. Liaison is also maintained with local officers of the Nature Conservancy, who are interested in a number of sites (mainly at reservoirs or along the less used rural canals) which have been formally scheduled as Sites of Special Scientific Interest—usually in regard to the conservation of rare species of fauna or flora.

It is in the nature of running an artificial waterway through other people's property that claims or complaints—usually of a minor yet not unimportant nature—continually arise on such matters as seepage, flooding, fencing defects, boundary problems and the like. These may require both investigation on the site itself and also a study of the statutory or other relationships governing the Board's liability in the matter. Thus seepage or flooding may be found to have occurred not from the canal but from a water-course whose maintenance is not the responsibility of the Board. At the same time reference to the enabling Act may reveal that the landowner himself has responsibilities of which he is totally unaware. Sometimes, too, the provisions of the Act may have been rendered meaningless by some change of circumstances that has since occurred. Thus the liability to provide fencing to prevent cattle straying along the towpath is totally inappropriate in an area which has long since been built up, or where a factory may now occupy a site where a miller formerly had certain water rights. Invariably, therefore, these matters require prompt and thorough investigation. For every one that gives rise to a claim for or against the Board or some other form of public or private 'row', there are many others which are promptly and quietly settled to the satisfaction of both parties. But this would not be so if there did not exist the organization to deal with cases as they arose.

Legal Services

There is a complex statutory background. There are some 600 local Acts extending back over 200 years yet constantly relevant to the present day. The work of the Board's solicitor is at once specialized in some respects and widely ranging in others. Apart from the volume of work on conveyancing, litigation and general advice, an aspect of particular importance is the study of existing and new legislation affecting individual canals or the system as a whole. Government legislation and the private Bills introduced by other statutory undertakers require detailed and expert examination to consider their impact on the Board's rights and interests.

Some Useful Addresses

British Waterways Board
Melbury House
Melbury Terrace
London
NW1 6JX

Great Ouse Restoration Society
(Hon. Secretary: D. J. Kettle)
8 Manor Road
Kempston
Bedford

Inland Waterways Association
114 Regent's Park Road
London
NW1 8UQ

Kennet and Avon Canal Trust Ltd.
(Hon. Secretary: D. D. Hutchings)
The Coppice
Elm Lane
Lower Earley
Reading
Berks

Lower Avon Navigation Trust Ltd.
'Gable End'
The Holloway
Pershore
WR10 1HW

Linton Lock Supporters' Club
(Hon. Secretary: I. B. Close)
'Rosehurst'
Great Ouseburn
York
YO5 9RJ

The National Trust
Stratford Canal Office
Lapworth
Solihull
Warwickshire

Peak Forest Canal Society Ltd.
(General Secretary: E. Keaveney)
35 Councillor Lane
Cheadle
SK8 2HU

Pocklington Canal Amenity Society
(Hon. Secretary: Mrs. S. M. Nix)
74 Westminster Road
York
YO3 6LY

Upper Avon Navigation Trust Ltd.
Avon House
Harvington
Worcestershire

Waterway Recovery Group
4 Wentworth Court
Wentworth Avenue
Finchley
London
N3 1YD

Yorkshire Derwent Trust Ltd.
(Hon. Secretary: Dr. G. H. Smith)
24 The Moorway
Tranmere Park
Guiseley
LS20 8LB

Bibliography and further reading

Periodicals

The most valuable sources of published information have been past issues of:
> Bulletin of the Inland Waterways Association
> Navvies (formerly Navvies Notebook)

and I am particularly grateful to the IWA and the Waterway Recovery Group respectively for making complete sets of each available for study.

Other periodicals I have consulted are:

Waterways World
Motor Boat and Yachting
Small Boat
Waterways News   British Waterways Board
Avon News   Lower Avon Navigation Trust Ltd.
Cut and Trust   Stratford-upon-Avon Canal Society
> Progress reports of the Upper Avon Navigation Trust Ltd.
The Butty   Kennet and Avon Canal Trust Ltd.
The Lock Gate   Great Ouse Restoration Society
Caldon News   Caldon Canal Society
> Newsletter of the Peak Forest Canal Society Ltd.
Cuttings   Shropshire Union Canal Society Ltd.
Double Nine   Pocklington Canal Amenity Society

Books and pamphlets—general and historical

Annual Reports of the British Waterways Board
Remainder Waterways—A report to the Secretary of State for the Environment by the Inland Waterways Amenity Advisory Council, 1971
The Facts About the Waterways, BWB, 1965
The Last Ten Years, BWB, 1973

Charles Hadfield, *British Canals*, David and Charles, Newton Abbot, 4th edition, 1970

Charles Hadfield (general editor), *Canal Enthusiasts' Handbook No. 2*, David and Charles, Newton Abbot, 1973

Robert Aickman, *Know Your Waterways*, G. Dibb Ltd., Norwich, 6th edition

Charles Hadfield, *The Canals of the East Midlands*, David and Charles, Newton Abbot, 2nd edition, 1970

Charles Hadfield, *The Canals of the West Midlands*, David and Charles, Newton Abbot, 2nd edition, 1969

Charles Hadfield, *The Canals of South Wales and the Border*, David and Charles, Newton Abbot, 2nd edition, 1967

Charles Hadfield and John Norris, *Waterways to Stratford*, David and Charles, Newton Abbot, 2nd edition, 1968

Brochure of the National Festival of Boats and Arts, Stratford-upon-Avon, IWA, 1964

Kenneth R. Clew, *The Kennet and Avon Canal*, David and Charles, Newton Abbot, 2nd edition, 1973

Ray Denyer, *Introducing the Kennet and Avon Canal*, Kennet and Avon Canal Trust Ltd., Reading, 1971

Crofton Beam Engines, the Crofton Society

Brochure of the Rally of Boats at the Reopening of the Stourbridge Canal, Staffordshire and Worcestershire Canal Society, 1967

Dudley Canal Tunnel, Dudley Canal Trust, 1973

Leslie Hales and John Pyper (edited by), *The 'Old Union' Canals of Leicestershire and Northamptonshire*, The Old Union Canals Society, 2nd edition, 1970

Margaret E. Richards, *A History of the Navigation of the Great Ouse Between Bedford and St. Ives* (supplement to *The Lock Gate*), Great Ouse Restoration Society, 1969

Dorothy Summers, *The Great Ouse*, David and Charles, Newton Abbot, 1973

D. Ripley, *The Peak Forest Tramway*, Oakwood Press, Lingfield, 2nd edition, 1972

A. Rimmer, *The Cromford and High Peak Railway*, Oakwood Press, Lingfield, 5th edition, 1970

James Eyles, *Cruising Along the Mon. and Brec. Canal*, Starling Press Ltd., Newport, 1972

Books and pamphlets—navigational and descriptive

Nicholson's Guides to the Waterways: South-east, North-west, South-west, North-east, BWB, 1971-3

L. A. Edwards, *Inland Waterways of Great Britain*, Imray Laurie Norie and Wilson, St. Ives, Hunts, 5th edition, 1972

Heather Salter (editor), *The Canals Book 73*, Link House Publications Ltd., Croydon, 1973

Gateway to the Avon, Lower Avon Navigation Trust Ltd., Pershore, 7th edition, 1971

Stratford-upon-Avon Canal Guide, Stratford-upon-Avon Canal Society, Leamington Spa, 4th edition, 1973

Jean Hall and Joy Yeates, *The Grand Western Canal* (leaflets Nos. one and two), Devon County Council, Exeter

Alan Jeffery, *The Caldon Canal*, Caldon Canal Society

The Brecon and Abergavenny Canal—A Cruising Map and Guide, BWB

Robert Shopland, Charles Smith (editors), *Inland Waterways Guide to Holiday Hire*, IWA/Boat World Publications, 1973

Acknowledgments

I owe a great debt of gratitude to many people involved in water-way restoration, for I claim no extensive personal experience of restoring waterways. Although, on the one hand, many years of interests in and cruising on inland waterways and, on the other, many years of helping to revive and run the semi-voluntary Festiniog Railway (see *Railways Revived*) have provided an insight into the problems likely to be encountered. Nevertheless, those who have made of waterway restoration their own private world could easily have resented a stranger's blundering in—but they have in fact been most friendly and helpful. I am particularly grateful for the assistance of the following:

General:
Inland Waterways Association   J. Dodwell, J. C. Heap
Waterway Recovery Group   G. Palmer
British Waterways Board   E. H. Arnold

Particular waterways:
Lower Avon   C. D. Barwell, I. M. Beard, R. Burrowes, D. C. B. Matthews, R. Sankey Smith
Stratford Canal   C. B. Grundy, David Hutchings, A. G. Johnson, A. Wagstaffe
Upper Avon   C. B. Grundy, David Hutchings
Kennet and Avon Canal   D. D. Hutchings, G. Lloyd
Grand Western Canal   D. C. Harward, C. V. Lucas
Wyken Arm   H. R. Dunkley
Stourbridge Canal   J. A. Robbins, G. Whittaker
Dudley Canal   O. W. Pinfold
Welford Arm   M. Bower
Great Ouse   J. S. Bissett, D. K. Cassels, N. Smith
Caldon Canal   B. Haskins, R. Savage

Ashton Canal   E. Keaveney
Lower Peak Forest Canal   B. Haskins, E. Keaveney
Buxworth Basin   Mrs. P. J. Bunker
Cromford Canal (Cromford to Ambergate section)   L. Bradley,
   H. Crossley
Great Northern Basin   E. G. Harrison
Brecon and Abergavenny Canal   J. Kegie, G. Lloyd, T. F. G.
   Young
Montgomery Canal   B. Haskins, R. Johnstone, M. H. Roberts
Linton Lock Navigation   I. B. Close
Yorkshire Derwent   D. C. North, G. H. Smith
Pocklington Canal   E. Lount

Appendix two is reproduced by kind permission of the British Waterways Board.

Duncan Calkin has kindly prepared the sketches on the title page and pages 5 and 7.

Maps (except No. 1) are based upon the Ordnance Survey Map with the sanction of the Controller of H.M. Stationery Office, Crown copyright reserved.

I am grateful to my wife Elisabeth for typing the manuscript of the text. But for her assistance, it would probably have been ready for the publisher in about 1980.

Index

Bold type indicates principal references, which should be consulted first.